31 Days To Paradise

31 Days To Paradise

CREATING THE MARRIAGE YOU DREAMED ABOUT

Dr. Donald M. Minter
Laura D. Minter

Columbus, Ohio

31 Days To Paradise

CREATING THE MARRIAGE YOU
DREAMED ABOUT

Don and Laura

It is often said the 'school of hard knocks' is the only school that really teaches. If that is the case, then Don and Laura have learned much during their almost four decades of marriage. Theirs is no fairytale relationship, instantaneous and perfect, a journey free of chaos and pain. To the contrary, it's more like the classic Hallmark movie, lives interrupted by difficulties and challenges, hanging on by fingernails, only to find redemption and healing as the movie draws to a close, paradise found. Yeah, probably a lot like the life you are going to live over the next few decades of married life.

Thankfully, just like the Hallmark classic, their journey has ended well, really well, more in love and passionate about each other than at any other time in their marriage which is saying a lot, given they are knocking on the door of 60 years on this spinning ball. Laura has somehow merged a demanding career with raising three boys and finding time to genuinely focus on the needs and wants of her husband. Likewise, Don, a pastor for almost 40 years in little churches across the country, has found some way to keep Laura the primary focus of his life.

However, make no mistake, the journey has been anything but painless and carefree. As you would expect, life, plain old ordinary life, has thrown more than a few curveballs their way, some of which you will learn about in the pages to follow. Nonetheless, the illusive glue all couples yearn to find, was discovered clinging to the pages of Ephesians 5, a timeless fount of advice straight from the mind of God, designed to bring abundant life for those in it for the long haul, those who believe

Pastor Don and Laura Minter

the fairytale can come true.

One last thing, the Minters are well, how shall we say it, rather 'out there' in their openness about marriage, life and, dare we even say it, sex! So don't be surprised if you blush here and there. You are married now. Time to be all grown up, for all-out 'adulting' to begin. Enjoy this 31-day journey. After all, it's always about the journey...

Dr. Jeren Rowell President Nazarene Theological Seminary

The first words I heard Don Minter speak were, "Hey, is that a weddin' band?" (insert Jersey accent). Don had just arrived at Northwest Nazarene College in Nampa Idaho where we were both students in philosophy and religion. Seeing my new, shiny wedding band, having just been married a few weeks, Don reached out to me as another newly married college student. That conversation began a nearly 40-year relationship between the Rowells and Minters. We soon learned that Don and Laura were the kind of people willing to be ruthlessly truthful about the challenges of growing a vibrant marriage. Those early days were filled with lots of conversations about how in the world we were going to navigate this sacred covenant without killing each other. In this candid and practical book, Don and Laura are providing those conversations, now from the perspective of a lifetime of wisdom and experience. These lessons will be helpful to those just beginning the journey of marriage, but those of us on down the trail can continue to learn from this teaching as well.

So who should read this book? Seasoned vets or newlyweds?

Paradise is always a work in progress. And maintenance is just as critical as brand new structures.

This project began as a primer for newlyweds, an introduction to their first 31 days of married life following the honeymoon. With that in mind, we invited married couples to critique the work as we posted each principle one day at a time in a private Facebook group.

Surprisingly, we began to hear murmuring, "This isn't just for beginners, it's a great reminder for those of us who have been married for any amount of time!" Then we began getting emails and comments about the relevance of this work for all married couples, a refresher course of sorts for those actively engaged in the effort to not only build paradise but also sustain it. Our audience grew unexpectedly as the married folks suggested the work was helping them to revitalize their marriage.

Thus, we offer this work as both a primer for newlyweds and a refresher course for those of you deep into the journey of paradise building. It may indeed serve as a reminder of what this thing we call marriage is really all about. Understand, it is never too late to build paradise.

We'd love to hear from you, if you find this book helpful, as you begin the journey or as a refresher for those of you deep into the quest for paradise. We would especially love to connect and celebrate with those of you who have found marriage to be everything God promised it could be.

Send your comments to revminter@me.com.

To our boys...

Raising three young men is a daunting task, almost as daunting as marriage itself. And like marriage, parenting is a learned art form, requiring experience and wisdom acquired on the fly. Unfortunately, Dustin and Derek, you grew up in a home being built by rookies, two young lovers, trying to figure out what married life and parenting was supposed to look like. Rest assured, we did our best...

Michael, our late surprise, walked into the home of two seasoned vets, a mom and dad who had survived the trauma and drama of the first two. Unfortunately, Michael, we were tired vets, tinkering on the verge of retirement from parenting duties. You, too, can rest assured we did our best...

This book is our effort to pass along the wisdom we were garnering on the fly. Much in the pages to follow you simply experienced as mom and dad were building paradise as best we knew how. Our hope is that this book will help all three of you do even better than we did when that special someone finally arrives in your life. Paradise is always worth the effort!

We knew one day all three of you would exit to chase your own dreams, to built your own paradise. Here you will find our experiences to help you find the paradise we all desire. Know this, we hammered out our own version of paradise. Mom and Dad love each other more now than we ever have. Likewise, our love for each of you has grown with each passing year.

Long after we are gone, our dream is that each of you can still chat with us in the pages of this book. Never give up on paradise. It's just around the corner...

Look Before You Leap
(if you can)

YOU'VE HEARD THE old adage, "Look before you leap," wisdom that ought to be implemented whenever possible. However, some things in life, including marriage, defy the ability to genuinely *look* before you leap, to really know what you're getting into before you step off the ledge, jump out of the plane, free fall into paradise (or hell). Sometimes, like it or not, the only way to really *look* is to *jump*, even when you're not quite sure where or how you're going to land. Welcome to the educated blind leap we call marriage. It is the most important decision you will ever make. But let's not pretend it is anything other than a courageous blind leap of faith into an unknown future. Your constant evolution as a person, like your spouse, almost guarantees this will be a risky jump, regardless of how well prepared you really are, even after all the pre-marriage and personality tests you may have taken to prepare. Inevitably, you will change and so will your spouse, relentlessly creating the necessity of adjustments, sometimes radical adjustments.

Such is the folly of living together first, as if marriage resembles *living together* in any way other than a shared address, a bed, and bills you are both mutually now responsible. Commitment changes everything, yes, everything. And, for those of you who thought you were doing the wise thing by practicing first, you will quickly discover your practice time, those glorious days of sharing time and space before signing on the dotted line, did surprisingly little to prepare you for the anticipated bliss of paradise awaiting those who dare to sign on the dotted line conveniently provided by your state of choice; of course, that assumes you survive your trial run which the vast majority never do (thus, ultimately learning how to fail rather than succeed). Somehow, once signed, everything changes in the blink of an eye, even if it takes you some time to discover your partner of choice has suddenly become your glued appendage for life (minus the miracle of divorce, society's painful and expensive solution for those unsuccessful in learning how to find and live in paradise, once attached at the hip).

The problem, of course, is the dotted line, the signed and delivered contract, altering the very nature of your relationship in the most profound ways imaginable. Sure, you may be living in the same space as before, still eating with the same person you have eaten with hundreds of times previous, but something has radically changed. You can't quite put your finger on it, but different it is. And you're not quite sure the change is a good one. Nope, the colors on the wall are still the same. The couch is in the usual spot. Your fiancé, that person you couldn't live without 24 hours earlier, hasn't suddenly turned into Godzilla, but, and this is important, he or she has morphed into your spouse, and something is radically different. You are just a bit uneasy but too far gone to reconsider. You are now airborne, out the door of that safe airplane called singleness, free falling toward paradise, terrified your parachute will fail to open. Once airborne, actually married, there is no turning back. Fall you must, like it or not. Learning to land is a mandatory skill set for everyone crazy enough to exit a perfectly good airplane.

Now comes the reality, the unexpected consequence of signing on the dotted line, everything altered slightly just by the mere act of committing: These first 31 days will remind you over and over again you simply can't go back to the good ole days, the way things used to be. You are now actually married, tethered at the hip in some miraculous way, committed.

The key is to make sure there's lots of rope to run with as you and your partner journey through life tied together (more on that later).

So take a deep breath, relax, and begin the journey meant to last a lifetime. These first 31 days may be the most important of all, the foundation upon which a lifetime of journeying together will be built. I have discovered over the past four decades of dating and then marriage (and working with countless couples trying to figure it all-out), the first year, surprisingly, is often the hardest. I suspect the difficulty arises out of false expectations as you enter an unforeseen paradise of another kind, a paradise rooted in reality, not some heartwarming Hallmark movie, not even the nirvana you created in your own mind.

Over the next 31 days, Laura and I will try to share from our own walk (ok, free fall) into our less-than-perfect paradise, as we attempted to first understand and then live out the wisdom God laid out in Ephesians Chapter 5. I imagine you will soon discover every paradise is not quite the one you expected, the one you created in your mind long before the realities of your married life began to appear. But, be of good cheer, paradise is built and cared for by couples wise enough to engage in the art of paradise building (Genesis 1:28-30). Paradise never just appears. It has to be built, one brick at a time. Savvy couples understand early on Paradise Requires Careful Planning, Building, And Maintenance. Fortunately, God anticipated the pitfalls awaiting every venture into paradise building, and so our journey begins by turning our attention to God's guidelines for creating your paradise. And yes, they are just suggestions, mere pointers on how to get it done, one step at a time. They are guiding principles, not a finalized blueprint, every couple can follow. Laura and I will offer some lessons from the School of Hard Knocks along the way. But, in the end, only the two of you and the Spirit of the Serving King can usher you into paradise. Marriage is always a 'build-as-you-go' endeavor.

We will explore four key dimensions toward building a thriving marriage, your own paradise and creating the partnership God envisioned for you:

- <u>The Foundation:</u> The Art of Mimicking (Ephesians 5:1-2)
- <u>The Unexpected Glue:</u> The Art of Sexuality (Ephesians 5:3-14)
- <u>The Normal Pattern:</u> The Art of Mutual Submission (Ephesians 5:15-21)
- <u>Conflict Resolution:</u> The Art of War (Ephesians 5:22-33)

As of this writing, Laura and I have been married 39 years. Year one was really not very much fun. We were two self-absorbed young adults (18 and 19), clueless as to what we had just gotten ourselves into, ill-prepared for a life of love. The next six years were full of adventure as we figured some things out, finally settling into a comfortable routine with all the energy and zeal of 20-somethings. Year 7 was chaos. Job changes, evolution into actual adults, and the ultimate test, raising children. Years 8-14 were child-centered (a horrible mistake) leading to a catastrophic year 15, hanging on by sheer determination of the will to love as we had pledged in that demanding promise to God and each other so many years ago. Miraculously, and I mean miraculously, two very wounded 30-somethings discovered love again, no not 'agapé' (that glue never abandoned us), rather 'phileo' and 'eros', an amazing passion sweeping us into what has now been a glorious 25 years as lovers and friends. We are always quick to share with folks it hasn't always been this way. Three years of our 39 were painful, even crushing at times. But that leaves 36 years of happiness and joy. And yes, over the last 25 years (onward from year 15), it has been flat out spectacular, just shy of paradise.

One last thing as you begin this journey, it is important to ask a critical question, "What kind of marriage do you want to create in the days ahead?" Perhaps, it's just survival, the privilege of saying we made it, hung in there in spite of how miserable we were. Or, better yet, the good life, great roommates and parents, happy for the most part, a very pleasant and meaningful marriage. But some of you may be after the proverbial 'whole ball of wax', the abundant life filled with passion and all the amazing benefits a great marriage can provide. For those of you chasing the whole ball of wax, this book is for you. Our suggestions are primarily for those zealots, the crazies, the naives who believe marriage can really be a passionate love affair across the decades, sex and all. No, not every moment, sometimes not even every year (baby years are brutal!), but comprehensively, yes, very yes!

It is for the zealots this book was written. Our hope is that you will exercise these principles early on in your relationship and across the passing decades. By implementing these principles early in the journey, you will avoid the 'humdrum' seeming to overtake so many marriages, robbing them of the passion and zeal God intends. Keep in mind, as well, this book is descriptive (how we implemented the principles of God) and not prescriptive (and so should you). You will have to design your own blueprint, your own way of 'being and doing' as a couple. Understand, no two couples are ever exactly alike. We will provide you with what we believe to be governing biblical principles, but you will have to figure out the particulars for applying those principles within your unique marriage. For those who do the work, the really hard work of relationship building, you are in for a journey of intimacy and friendship like none other, only attained by those who hang in there for the long haul. There is only one way to experience the ultimate marriage relationship: Hard Work Over A Sustained Period Of Time.

Let us suggest you engage this book during your first few months of marriage (maybe right after your passionate honeymoon, those first 31 days). The key will be spending a few moments each day talking about the implications of what you are discovering. For us, that usually means going for a walk, taking a drive, or settling in over a steaming hot cup of coffee. Whatever works for you, find a way to grab time daily, talk about the implications and usefulness of what you uncover, and watch where God takes you through the transformation unfolding in each of you.

First, read the 5th chapter of Ephesians in its entirety. But resist the temptation to read this book in big chunks, unless you want a quick overview before carefully moving forward one day at a time. Instead, read a section at a time, one principle each day. Then take a few minutes to think about how you might apply what you have just discovered. What would the principle look like if you applied to your specific marriage relationship? Finally, grab some couple time to chat about the insights you have gained. Your conversations will be the real jewels of this process as you dream together.

And, just in case you are wondering, this is a 31-day journey you will want to repeat as the years roll on; perhaps, even a yearly refresher. Timely tuneups go a long way toward preventing chaos down the line. Time to get to work. We are rooting for you...

CHAPTER 1

The Foundation: The Art of Mimicking

I 'M NOT POSITIVE about this, but I think I have been married to at
least six different women, maybe seven, each of them named Laura
DaForno, and each of them fondly familiar and yet shockingly
different. Most of the models I have enjoyed for the most part. However,
truth be told, version three, or maybe it was four, I would have preferred
to skip; but, then again, each model seems to have played an important
role in the fabulous woman I am married to today. My favorite is the
latest model. She seems to have been miraculously custom-made just for
me. Most of the rough edges were painfully ground off years ago by life's
relentless pursuit of improvement to all those journeying on the spinning
ball. It's no surprise after four decades of married life cascading around
in life's grand tumbler, the latest model has a glorious sheen only possible
after years of its best efforts at polishing. And yes, marriage is the best of
all tumblers, polishing those who remain to a brilliant sheen. But, boy,
has the ride been a wild one as both of us evolved into the latest models
of who we are. I suspect she has been married to at least that many men as
well (but she will have to fill you in on that).

Marriage, like life, is a learned art, relentless evolving, mandating a watchful and creative eye as the ever-changing reality breaks over the horizon. Thus, any book on marriage has to be about art, a developing landscape inclusive of the reality no two paintings (marriages) will ever be the same. But there are basic principles every couple will need, if they are to succeed in painting paradise (or hell for those unskilled in the art of marriage).

Like all things pertaining to life, marriage requires a great deal of skill and grace, more than we could have ever imagined. But at 19, the ripe old age of my decision to marry (Laura was 18), I had absolutely no idea what I was getting myself into. Worse yet, I had no understanding of just how seriously God took marriage (not unusual for young people raised in the inaugural generation of divorce for any and every reason). It would be several years later before I would really get a grasp on just what I had gotten into, and only then after a wise, old 50-something (hmmm, exactly what I am now) sat me down for an unwanted heart-to-heart about marriage and what it would take to survive. His advice, incredibly naive and dated (so said my brilliant 20-something-year-old brain), struck me as ill-advised and poorly suited for the 21st century. Still, I was desperate, and sinking fast into a marriage painted just like you would expect from two 20-something, first-born know-it-alls; and our painting was getting less and less attractive by the day. Frankly, we were creating a relational train wreck, paint thrown everywhere, the canvas a chaotic mess. Who knew painting a marriage was going to be such hard work.

Thinking he would need all the data, the dirt of why Laura was not fulfilling her end of the bargain, he stopped me midway through my opening diatribe. "Save it, all you are doing is creating your job description (a phrase I have never forgotten, as I share it with countless individuals painting their spouse in the worse possible light). Let's talk about the man you need to be to provide the healing for your bride God intended." Wow, I was not expecting that. And with that, my life as husband began to radically evolve. The transformation is not complete yet, but I think I may be heading into the final stage at the ripe old age of 58.

Ephesians 5 is the description of the journey that began to unfold in the days which followed. The first step (Ephesians 5:1) is rooted in the critical concept of *Radical And Extreme Equality*. It is the foundation upon which all Christian theology is built: *The Doctrine Of The Trinity*. It suggests nothing more, nothing less, than extreme equality between the three persons of the Trinity. Hence, there is no boss, no dictator, no supreme ruler, rather three Persons, one in nature, profoundly equal in every way; a recipe for disaster if there ever was one, unless they truly love one another in a self-sacrificial manner, each valuing the other more than self. Such is the doctrine of the Trinity and the intended foundation for every marriage relationship seeking to find paradise.

Radical Trinitarian Equality offers a working model essential for most (perhaps every) marriage relationships. It suggests the creation of a marriage model mimicking the operational framework within the Trinity, a functional and harmonious relationship template based on an understanding of two human beings who are equal, but uniquely damaged. Understand, human beings are never, and I mean never, equal; rather, they are uniquely created with strengths and weaknesses, each typically out of balance due to our fallen human nature, a story for another day. Hence, by pointing to 'radical equality', we are not suggesting equal in every detail; instead, an equality of *personhood* and worth before God.

But comprehending *radical equality* will not get the job done; rather, only a well executed methodology can carry you to the finish line. *Radical equality* will provide the foundation, but the hard work of exercising that equality in the day-to-day messiness of married life will require a great deal of education and effort. Thus, the necessity of this little primer provided to me in shell form some 30-plus years ago.

The secret comes in the form of *Imitation*, learning to mimic the life of Christ. Hence, our journey begins in Ephesians 5:1 and the biblical call to imitation. Rest assured, this will be the hardest work you have ever attempted. But for those who succeed, who learn how to mimic His self-sacrifice for the sake of another, the rewards are immense. Time to man-up or woman-up, as the case may be, and begin a life of imitation. Hang on tight, this will require more of you than you could have ever imagined. Let's get started...

Therefore be imitators of God...
Ephesians 5:1

" *Marriage may be the closest thing to Heaven or Hell any of us will know on this earth.*
—*Edwin Louis Cole*

Principle 1

Those who mimic divine love unleash a powerful life giving force upon their marriage.

I (Don) was one of the seemingly rare and fortunate ones reared in a happy home, never considering the idea my parents would not always be together. The thought literally never crossed my mind. Nor did I have any idea I was growing up in paradise, La La Land, known to only a privileged few. Divorce, the ravaging disease of the decades to follow, was still in its infancy, newly birthed in a culture determined to ease the pain of marriages gone south, hell on earth. Now in their late 70s, my parents, just as in love as they were on the day of their marriage, still hold hands, get loud and cantankerous with each other, and, if the occasional grin is to be believed, still chase each other around the bedroom every now and then (I sure hope so...gives me something to look forward to over the next two decades). So comes the challenge to *mimic* their success, to learn from seasoned professionals how to emulate a marriage well done. Their marriage was intentional, a well-thought-out plan implemented across the decades following their secret elopement (equally well planned out), two lovers on a mission to *mimic* a specific approach to marriage.

The challenge to *mimic*, well-tested ways of *being and doing*, His ways, is nothing new. Marriage, more than any other facet of life, is meant to be a reflection, a mimicking, of the Divine relationship operational within the Trinity (Father, Son, and Holy Spirit). But you cannot mimic what you don't know. So, the better your knowledge of their relationship (Father, Son, and Holy Spirit), the better your chance of reflecting their characteristics in your marriage relationship. Hence, the term Paul employs here is *mimetai* (the root of our English term mimic), meaning to copy the behavior of another and, in this case, the behavior of Jesus. Sounds easy enough. But for those who know the story well, the earthly life of Jesus doesn't end particularly well (He dies a brutal death on a cross). Thus, the challenge to mimic His behavior as the footing for every marriage relationship can be a bit intimidating for those thinking marriage is the gateway toward relational bliss (i.e., my spouse is going to be fully committed to making me happy). If you have been married for more than 24 hours, you have more than likely discovered both of you entered into marriage with the same mindset, "My partner can't wait to make me happy!" And, in some sense, that ought to be the case, is the case.

First, a quick word about the Trinity and the equality of each member of the Godhead (Father, Son, and Holy Spirit). Their relationship rests on a foundation of profound *equality*; meaning, in the most real way possible, neither the Father, nor the Son, nor the Spirit, has any advantage over the other. Theirs is a relationship of profound equality. Imagine how dangerous a relationship of true equality could become! Consider the potential for some knock-down, drag-out wars! Not to mention the tragedy of collateral damage if the Trinity declared war. Thus, the Persons of the Trinity model functionally different roles within their relationship of extreme equality. Jesus, in the midst of His most difficult moments in life, announces to all the world He will willingly surrender to the will of the Father, "Father, if You are willing, remove this cup from Me. Nevertheless, not My will, but Yours, be done" (Luke 22:42). Here we discover the essential and liberating piece of self-surrender: *Equality Enables Self-Surrender Out Of A Sense Of Genuine Concern For What Is Best For Another* (specifically, your spouse). The tricky part is a genuine concern for others above 'self'.

Our essential 'self' has a bad habit of mandating "Me first!" more times than we would like to admit; hence, the need for some assistance, a power capable of overcoming 'self'. Such is provided for us via the indwelling presence and power of the Holy Spirit. More on that later...

I confess that early in our relationship I was poorly equipped for the whole business of mimicking the sacrificial life of Jesus. Oh sure, if a terrorist threatened her life, I would like to believe I would be 'Johnny on the spot' but genuinely considering her needs first in the mundane (and, wow, is there a lot of mundane) of everyday life is a whole different ballgame.

Laura has suffered from a thyroid condition for over 25 years. Amongst the many side effects is an almost complete inability to remain comfortable in any extreme temperature (any temp below 78° and above 80°). Unfortunately, my thyroid functions just fine. Thus, the war of the household thermostat constantly threatens to erupt especially at night, as my naked body sweats on top of the covers while she burrows into the ever-growing pile of covers thrown her way, trying to find enough warmth to survive the arctic nights of 68°! Now, here is the hilarity in our dilemma. Both of us are radically committed to surrendering our needs for the sake of the other. She freezes (the temps push 75° when Michael and I are gone), and I sweat (windows cracked open even in the winter anytime we are apart). But, hot or not, my hand softly lands on her derrière as she softly purrs as we quietly slip into Never Never Land. No better feeling in all the world than to peacefully sleep in the sacrificial love of your spouse.

Those who learn to mimic self-surrender for the sake of another soon discover a profound secret: *Life Is Resurrected When Given For The Sake Of Another*. As the Son gave His life to the will of the Father, so the Father bestowed resurrection and life to the Son. Resurrection and life are just around the bend for those who learn to mimic self-surrender for the sake of their cherished spouse. Discovering the joy of resurrected life is one of the glorious fruits of married life. It's the unexpected 'gold mine' within self-sacrifice...

Time for coffee and conversation...

- What does authentic equality mean to you as you think about being married?
- Why does radical equality create a willingness to sacrifice for another?
- How would you define personal sacrifice?

Action Point...

- How might you live sacrificially for your spouse in the mundaneness of life?
- Thank your spouse for one of the ways they sacrifice for you (be specific).

...as beloved children.
Ephesians 5:1

" Being deeply loved by someone gives you strength, while loving someone deeply gives you courage. —Lao Tzu

Principle 2

Those who know they are loved are capable of incredible sacrifice for another.

I suspect there is no greater power in the universe than the power of being genuinely loved by another. As Lao Tzu suggested, it provides courage to even the weakest. This is never more true than in a marriage relationship empowered by a profound love for one another. But the term here in Ephesians arrives unexpectedly, replacing the normative *phileo* (from which we get Philadelphia, city of brotherly love), typically associated with love within a family unit, 'feelings' of affection generated by family relationships. In its place is the surprising term *agapé*, a term reserved to describe the love operational in the life of Jesus. Specifically, *agapé* describes a love in which concern for another overrides any concern for self. Hence, Jesus surrenders His life for the sake of those He values above His own: *You.* But *agapé* operates independently of mere feelings; instead, it's driven by a decision of the mind and will. Your decision to 'love' your partner ought to arise out of an intentional decision independent of the way you feel (and, true, some days you will not feel like 'loving'). Hence, weddings have employed a somewhat unexpected component for centuries: the vow.

Your wedding vows only work because they are rooted in a commitment rising up out of the mind and will rather than 'feelings'. Hence, weddings have historically been contractual in nature, a commitment, a promise to engage regardless of forthcoming conditions. Consider for a moment the extreme nature of the historical wedding vows: *Will you have this woman to be your wedded wife, to live together after God's ordinance in the holy estate of matrimony? Will you love her, comfort her, honor and keep her in sickness and in health; and forsaking all others, keep yourself only unto her, so long as you both shall live?* Followed by an equalling compelling pledge: *I, _____, take you, _____, to be my wedded husband/wife, to have and to hold from this day forward, for better–for worse, for richer–for poorer, in sickness and in health, to love and to cherish, till death us do part, according to God's holy ordinance; and thereto I pledge you my faith.* Notice how the promise to love (agapé) is couched in a setting in which the external conditions could rapidly go from great (for better) to flat out awful (for worse). And, of course, the ultimate pledge, "...till death us do part." A marriage relationship is typically rooted in a commitment, a contract, a binding covenant, between you and your partner intentionally free of any conditions rendering the contract null and void (even the 'out clause' suggested by Jesus, adultery, is the by-product of a 'hard heart').

As you have already discovered in life, feelings come and go, sometimes in a seemingly uncontrollable manner (more on this in a later section). Marriages dependent upon 'feelings of love' are always at risk, simply because 'feelings' too often have a mind of their own. Uncontrollable circumstances of life appear with little rhyme or reason. Someone gets very sick, a job is lost or a variety of other unforeseen circumstances. Many years back, Laura and I were acquainted with an adorable newlywed couple. They were picture book in every way, fairytale even, pretty people of the highest kind, both on the fast-track to career successes reserved for those fortunate few in life. Less than two years into their fairytale relationship, she discovered a life-altering physical condition the best specialists could not decipher, much less cure. In the mundane language of our day, she was becoming increasingly overweight. I remember thinking at the time this relationship is doomed. How will these kids sustain love and passion while enduring such drastic changes to her physical body? Twenty years later, their marriage continues to blossom. They have clearly figured out how to 'love' in all of its forms, as they have journeyed together through every 'better or worse'. And, yes, the weight is still there, and his hair is now long gone (just like mine!).

Consider for a moment the great sacrifices you made during the days of your dating experiences. Conversations deep into the night when you should have been sleeping. Long drives just to spend a little more time together. Lavish gifts you really couldn't afford. And the list goes on and on. Those who sense they are loved are capable of extreme sacrifice for the one who loves them deeply.

It still amazes me after all these years of married life, how much easier it is to lay down my life for my bride (in the mundane nonsense, like who gets to pick up our child from grandma's) when I know she loves me. Here is an important reminder for you as you step into the journey of married life: *Loving Your Spouse Is Not Enough, They Have To Know It.* Laura and I discovered early on our primary love language (the one we use to say I love you) was not the same. Hence, much of our "I love you" went unheard, wasted, lost to cyberspace. It would be years before either one of us felt truly loved, and, tragically, those who don't feel radically loved soon become unwilling to make the sacrifices necessary to sustain the highest levels of intimacy and trust. Laying a foundation of love for your spouse is essential in creating an environment where sacrifice is offered frequently for the sake of another. You will need this skill over and over again as you love across the decades (and love those little bundles God may provide later).

This will be the challenge for you and your partner: How to speak the right love language in the days ahead (more on this later). Most of us have a very bad habit of speaking our own love language rather than our partner's. Therefore, much of the love we communicate goes unnoticed and unregistered by the person who needs desperately to know how much we love them. As the circumstances encircling your life begin to change, sometimes for better, sometimes for worse, your spouse will need to know more than ever how radically committed you are to loving them...

Time for coffee and conversation...

- What external conditions are you most afraid will change in the years to come?
- Why does the knowledge you are loved enable you to sacrifice for your spouse?

Action Point...

- How might you reassure your spouse your love is unconditional, independent of the circumstances life throws your way? Do it now!
- Create a game plan to manage the circumstance your spouse is most afraid of.

Walk...
Ephesians 5:2

" *You never really understand a person until you consider things from his point of view... Until you climb inside of his skin and walk around in it.*
    —*Harper Lee (To Kill A Mocking bird)*

Principle 3

Marriage is a marathon. Stroll rather than sprint.

Dating, for the most part, is an all-out sprint, hormones raging, passions banging against the walls of self-constraint, sometimes even crashing over the walls (awkward for all of us trying to hold onto the glory of the wedding night). It's the body's way of proclaiming, "You might have a winner here!" Unfortunately, the body's biochemistry is a lousy 'picker' for the long haul. And the body, for all its early antics and all-out enthusiasm, often fizzles long before the race is over. So comes the warning to slow down, take a deep breath, and realize you have entered a marathon, a very long race across the decades of your life. And you can't run it alone. This is a life-long, three-legged race of the best (or worse) kind. More importantly, once the chase is over, the mating accomplished, the victory won, eros completed in all of its infant glory and awkwardness, your body, falling out of the hormonal stupor, has a tendency to quickly ask your spouse, "What else you got?" Rest assured, they better have something once the hormones have settled back into levels of normalcy or you are in for one long, painful journey. For this three-legged race, any idea of 'sprinting' needs to be left behind. Paul reminds us of the need to 'walk' carefully in the decades to come.

Like most of Paul's carefully chosen language, the verb here for 'walk' (*peripatéo*) suggests much more than simply going for a stroll along life's journey. To the contrary, it suggests a carefully thought-out manner of living. The verb is often translated as 'live' and reflects a deep concern for the moral concerns of life. Paul challenges those committed to 'loving' to do so in a manner reflecting the concerns of Jesus as He lived a life of love: *Enhancing The Life Of Another.*

But Paul's tone is equally forceful. The term is presented as a present active imperative, meaning not merely 'suggesting' a long walk mimicking the characteristics of 'love' (*agapé*); rather, he is commanding it as the foundation upon which every marriage relationship will find life and vitality. More to the point, the active voice suggests the subject (you) must purposely engage in the activity of love. It will not happen spontaneously. This 'walk' requires intentionality and effort of the highest kind, discipline beyond the norm. Once again, the challenge to 'love' is not rooted in feelings; instead, it is a purposeful decision to act 'lovingly' (for the sake of the other) across the decades of married life.

Most of us are fairly efficient at loving our spouses self-sacrificially while under the influence of raging hormones, the sprinting phase of the relationship (typically, the dating phase). But, sooner or later, those hormones return to balance, the sprint unintentionally becomes a walk as the patterns of marriage begin to settle in, reflecting the norms of who you are and how you live. Then, and often only then, do you finally and fully begin to realize your spouse is profoundly different than you had imagined. Normal hormonal levels slow us down, enabling us to take a deeper look at who we have married. Keep in mind, you have been journeying with a partner as stoked on hormones as you were. Alas, reality arrives for us all only at the conclusion of the dating phase (often within the first few months of marriage).

Now comes the opportunity to 'crawl into their skin', to really begin to comprehend just who you are walking with in this trek called marriage. Then the horrible moment of awakening we all dread as intimacy over the long haul begins to reveal '*full disclosure*' regarding the person you have married; physically, spiritually and every other dimension of what it means to be human. This new relationship, with its pledge to a life of togetherness, comes with revelations of all kinds as you 'walk', rather than sprint, across the days ahead. Thus, the dreaded moment of revelation, that unanticipated understanding: *Your Spouse Is Broken.* It is the unwanted moment of awareness in every marriage, "I have married a broken unit!" Hence, the command of Paul to "Keep walking!" Resist the temptation to stop, turn, and run!

A long 'walk' of love would be so much easier to prescribe, if we were all broken in the same ways. But, just like a human fingerprint, no two of us are ever broken in the exact same way. Hence, learning to walk in a healing and redemptive manner toward your spouse is always complicated. It is in that profound moment of understanding who your spouse really is that you begin to comprehend the complexity of learning how to 'walk' with them in such a way that it provides healing and redemption toward your wounded partner.

But, of course, you can't really know that until you have walked the proverbial "...mile in their shoes." Here comes the difficult part: getting out of your own shoes, leaving behind your way of doing things, and genuinely understanding their way. Fortunately, marriage has a way of providing keen insights into the heart, mind, and soul of your spouse, if, and only if, you are wise enough to slow down, give up the sprint, and walk carefully beside the person you have promised to stroll beside for the remainder of your days. Walk with your eyes wide open observing the ins and outs of this person you have pledged to love. Walk slow enough to really look, to genuinely understand your spouse, warts and all. You are the most powerful healing agent your spouse will ever know. Embrace the God-given opportunity to provide healing and transformation to your spouse. Slow down, soak it all in, and walk on for a lifetime...

Time for coffee and conversation...

- How well do you really know your spouse? What five goals in life matter most to them?
- How well do you know yourself? What five goals do you have for your life? Does your spouse know them?

Action Point...

- Describe your spouse to your spouse. Just how close did you get?
- Now, listen carefully to your spouse's understanding of who you are. Does your spouse really know you?

...in the way of love
Ephesians 5:2

" *Let there be spaces in your togetherness, and let the winds of the heavens dance between you. Love one another but make not a bond of love: Let it rather be a moving sea between the shores of your souls.* —*Kahlil Gibran*

Principle 4
Successful marriages learn to walk on all four legs instead of three.

Most of us have taken part in the proverbial three-legged race at one time or another. And truth be told, they are rarely graceful or efficient; rather, a painful exhibition of futility providing endless laughter for the spectators on the sidelines. The eventual winner has done nothing more than conquer equally pathetic racers. It is simply impossible to run gracefully tethered to the leg of another human being. Too often, marriage relationships become awkward three-legged racers trying to become 'one' in their journey through life. But 'oneness' is the by-product of learning to "walk in love" rather than learning to walk while 'tethered' to another human being. Hence, the critical importance of moving beyond the 'commitment' to function as one like three-legged racers and, instead, the development of a fluid relationship reflecting a 'one in nature', not in person. Thus, you can be very independent and still reflect the oneness of your nature as a couple, mimicking the nature of Father, Son, and Spirit, the Trinitarian model: one in nature, three in person.

Consider again, the Trinity, the ultimate equality of relationship, "Three persons, one in nature." For all of their oneness, and theirs is a oneness of intense proportions, a oneness reflecting extreme equality, there is still independence and authentic freedom. Jesus continually dialogues with the Father regarding the course of action needed in the coming moments, and yet, in every instance, He acts according to His own freewill, following authentic dialogue with the Father. Likewise, the Father, after consulting with the Son, liberates Him to act within His own autonomy. And it's critical to understand, they don't always see eye to eye.

A few days (years) ago, you were independent, free of obligation, able to choose any human being crossing your path. Yet, for some inexplicable reason, you chose your spouse to begin the journey of a lifetime. Something about your spouse captured you, drew you in, created an intense desire to spend the rest of your life together, and here you are, married. Too often, people seem to forget the creation of their spouse occurred, for the most part, independent of their influence. External forces, independent of you, shaped the person with whom you now journey. And believe it or not, it is important for those forces to continue to operate, even after marriage.

It is imperative that you resist the temptation to suddenly put a leash on your partner, stripping them of the marvelous influences shaping them in the first place. Those external forces created the dynamic person you have vowed to love. Trust those forces to continue to work as you become yet another force shaping the person your spouse will become. You are now a vital part of the process. Trust the process to continue to work as you contribute your unique influences.

Don and I were gifted three-legged runners in the early days of our marriage. Committed to 'oneness' we did almost everything together, even shopping expeditions which Don loathes to this very day. I love to bargain shop (when I have money!), and like all gifted shoppers, could spend hours in the local mall looking for deals too good to pass up. The challenge of finding that perfect gift for those I love is so invigorating! For Don, shopping, under any conditions, is nothing short of a visit to the local torture chamber. But, in the spirit of 'oneness', he was determined to shop gracefully tethered to me in a beautiful exhibition of three-legged racing. The results were glorious from his perspective. Because he loved God and me, he endured far too many hours of shopping (two or three, I think), when suddenly I announced he was banned from all future shopping expeditions. Yes, I fired him, terminated him in the nicest possible way. Our three-legged race had come to a crashing halt. It was probably one of the best decisions I ever made. And, thankfully, I have been liberated from the hideous task of shopping with a miserable man. We have fired each other from a good number of activities across the years.

But rest assured, there will be plenty of 'oneness' the two of you will discover making for wonderful three-legged racing. Don and I love to travel and often do. We have ventured out across the globe, racing together, delighted with all the adventures. We most often visit island destinations together, Europe, or some other exotic destination. But tonight, as I write these pages, Don and I are separated by 100 miles. Michael, our 12-year old, and Don have abandoned me to go skiing, one of their favorite three-legged activities as father and son. Meanwhile, I'm cozied up in my warm bed, temperature warmer than they would ever tolerate, delighted to have some alone time while the boys are off playing.

The "walk in love" recognizes some things ought to be done separately, independently, miles apart. Those things, in the end, build up your partner, refresh them, edify them in ways you never could. It is the secret of creating 'spaces in your togetherness', spaces allowing external forces to continue to shape the love of your life in ways you never could, energizing and invigorating your partner and your marriage for years to come.

There is a serendipity for those who discover the secret of creating 'spaces in your togetherness': *The Reunions.* I'm delighted when the happy and content man comes home. Space allows you to find genuine excitement again when reuniting with your partner. It is the bliss of honeymoons revisited throughout the course of a lifetime, the joy of encountering a genuinely refreshed and happy spouse. Go ahead, create spaces in your togetherness. Space is an important key to togetherness...

Time for coffee and conversation...

- What activities do the two of you genuinely enjoy together?
- What activities do the two of you prefer alone?

Action Point...

- Make a list of the things you will do together.
- Make another list of the things you will do apart.

...as Christ loved us.
Ephesians 5:2

" *As a single footstep will not make a path on the earth, so a single thought will not make a pathway in the mind. To make a deep physical path, we walk again and again. To make a deep mental path, we must think over and over the kind of thoughts we wish to dominate our lives.*

—*Henry David Thoreau*

Principle 5

Feelings always follow thinking.
Think well of your spouse.

Pastoring has a way of introducing you to a tremendous amount of bad press concerning the people whom God has called you to love. I often call it the most challenging dimension of pastoral ministry: loving folks whose dirty laundry you have been exposed to far too many times. I have spent years trying to shield my eyes from the dirty laundry clinging to the people I want to love as Jesus does. I have equally discovered it is the most potentially harmful dimension of an unending walk of love (marriage): you simply are exposed to way too much dirty laundry in the life of the person you are trying desperately to love. Exposure to dirty laundry is the unexpected consequence for those seriously engaged in a journey of relational intimacy, and it inevitably (and often unintentionally) creates '*collateral damage*': unwanted negative feelings toward your spouse. Here we discover the marriage killer: *Negative Images Generating Unwanted Feelings Quickly Taking Root.* Tragically, once the downward cycle begins, it often becomes a relentless spiral toward the death of your marriage.

Fortunately, Jesus reminds us how to love even in the midst of unwanted knowledge of dirty laundry. Consider carefully for a moment what Jesus really, I mean really, knows about you? How much garbage, ugly and smelly, has Jesus witnessed as you have pranced through life? Yet, in spite of all the ugliness Jesus knows about you, He continues to love you, to think well of you. Admit it, Jesus knows more than enough to have abandoned the love effort toward you long ago.

But in mimicking the ways of Jesus, we learn yet another vital dimension of the life of love: Think consistently well of those you intend to love across a lifetime. I'm pretty sure Jesus learned and modeled for us the art of loving the 'good, the bad, and the ugly' by simply framing each of us in the best possible light. Hence, Jesus focuses on the 'good' in us.

As you have already discovered in your journey, thinking well of others requires a great deal of discipline. Intimacy will not allow you to insulate yourself from 'dirty laundry' as you spend a lifetime with another person (more on the art of avoiding dirty laundry in the pages to follow). Fortunately, while the old saying may be true, "I can't unsee that," it is never the last word. Paul reminds us in Philippians of a more important truth guiding us into the ways of Jesus, a critical concept protecting, transforming, and redeeming any relationship, especially marriage!

Finally brothers, whatever is true, whatever is noble, whatever is right, whatever is pure, whatever is lovely, whatever is admirable — if anything is excellent or praiseworthy — think about such things. (Philippians 4:8)

Henry David Thoreau clearly thought along the same lines as the Apostle Paul, "To make a deep mental path, we must think over and over the kinds of thoughts we wish to dominate our lives." Therefore, if you wish positive images to dominate your mind regarding your spouse, you must think about them again and again. Yes, you must dwell on them, continually. It must be an never-ending cycle. It not only protects but can even heal the most damaged relationship.

I have acquired over 3,000 pictures of my bride stored away in my digital photo file. Almost every one is a good picture (Laura mandates I delete every bad one!). But I have taken at least twice that many deleted long ago from the file, forever banished, forbidden to ever see the light of day again.

Many of those Laura never saw. I deleted them before she caught sight of them. But I have five my bride grimaces at everytime she sees them. They are my five favorites, gloriously pasted on my laptop screen, photos of Laura in a bikini. I see them many times a day, a constant reminder of the incredible woman I call my bride. Truth be told, I have seen them so many times they have become a 'deep mental path', a rut, a well worn trail to the image I carry in my mind anytime I hear her name, Laura. My modest bride is horror stricken anytime I have my laptop open in public (and, yes, I live at coffee shops). But this is one battle she hasn't won. She gets it and has finally, reluctantly, relented, knowing how helpful it is for me to have deep mental ruts in my mind, always leading to wonderful images of my bride.

The '*tricksy*' part is taking responsibility for the way you think about your spouse. Far too often wounded partners roll into my office proclaiming an inability to control the way they think about their spouse. It is not the truth. To love as Jesus loves is to control what your mind contemplates regarding the person you are trying to love for a lifetime. Controlling the mind is a glorious by-product of life in the Spirit, mimicking the way of Jesus, imitating God. Learning to control the mind is an essential tool enabling positive feelings to manifest across a lifetime of marriage. It is His way of thinking.

But there is an unexpected delightful by-product of thinking well about your spouse: *Positive Feelings Take Root And Flourish.* Those who think well begin to experience seemingly uncontrollable feelings of love (*phileo* and even *eros*); but they are anything but uncontrollable. Feelings simply follow the deep-rutted mental paths we create in our minds. Feelings are the unexpected handmaidens of right thinking. Take seriously the challenge to think well of your spouse in the days ahead, and you will receive one of marriage's most precious gifts: warm, fuzzy feelings of love and passion as you journey onward together...

Time for coffee and conversation...

- What pictures do you carry around of your spouse that you see consistently?
- What traits do you really love about your spouse?
- How do you feel when you think about the positive aspects of your spouse?

Action Point...

- Find five favorite pictures of your spouse and plant them where you will repeatedly see them.
- Make of list of the positive things you need to consistently think about your spouse.
- Show your spouse your fabulous five pictures. Tell them why you love them.

...a fragrant offering.
Ephesians 5:2

“ *Sacrifice engulfed in the stench of bitterness was never really sacrifice at all; rather, just a pathetic slave sacrificed and left to rot at the altar of pretense.* —Don Minter

Principle 6

The stench of rotting self-sacrifice can ruin a marriage.

Dead fish left unattended stink. And sacrifice, giving your life for another, always has the potential to stink up the room, so I have discovered over these many years of marriage counseling. Here we stumble onto what may be the most difficult aspect of a lifelong journey of imitating the self-sacrificial life of love modeled by Jesus: sacrifice producing a pleasant, fragrant aroma. The potential for an unpleasant stench at the altar of self-sacrifice is immense.

Most of us have managed, through great discipline and fortitude, to sacrifice from time to time, an occasional offering for the sake of another human being. Typically, sacrifice is directed toward those we love, and care about most, even benefit from, folks like our spouse! But sacrifice often has an 'if-then' clause: "If I sacrifice, then this is the payoff I expect." The payoff is the anticipated reward for sacrifice, and most of us genuinely struggle with the concept of sacrifice without a payoff. Hence, most of our self-sacrifice is reciprocal in nature. And look out when the payoff doesn't arrive. The aroma of self-sacrifice begins to change, often quickly, rendering the effort futile, even detrimental to the marriage relationship. The stench of resentment begins to fill the air. Sadly, self-sacrifice in a marriage relationship can become nothing more than a stinky badge of honor creating more damage than healing.

Consider the sacrifice of Jesus for a moment, "For one will scarcely die for a righteous person — though perhaps for a good person one would dare even to die, but God shows His love for us in that while we were still sinners, Christ died for us" (Romans 5:7-8). Theologians have longed struggled to understand who Jesus died for; that is, did He die for only those who eventually repent and find new life, or did He also die for those whose lives never reflect the redemptive grace of God? If He died only for those who find redemption and healing, then His love reflects an 'if-then' clause. The end justifies the means. But, what if Jesus actually died for all of us? What if He laid down His life for the sake of all human beings, even the most notoriously rebellious and unrepentant? Let me suggest, He died for us all, even the most consistent sinner among us, and the aroma was a fragrant offering to God as He lovingly laid down His life, even for the 'unloveable'. But understand, His self-sacrifice is always, in every instance, every circumstance, intentional and purposeful. His sacrifice creates the optimum conditions in which redemption and healing can occur. Sacrifice doesn't guarantee redemption and healing; it merely creates the optimum conditions for healing to unfold. So comes the tremendously difficult challenge to lay down your life for the sake of your spouse, independent of the unseen aftereffect still over the horizon, intentionally creating optimum conditions for the best possible outcomes, yet absent of all guarantees. Sacrifice is an extremely risky endeavor in every relationship, especially marriage.

Chances are you have been reared in a cultural environment placing little value on the importance of self-sacrifice for the sake of undeserving others, especially a spouse. Ours is a culture mandating an immediate payoff. And marriage, like every other aspect of life, is defined as nothing more than a mutually beneficial arrangement. But those who engage in the effort to mimic Christlikeness in their marriage have entered into another value structure, one emphasizing a life of self-sacrifice for the sake of another. Christlikeness is an alternative culture, one where self-sacrifice for the sake the of another is the most fragrant of aromas.

Let me offer one last tidbit as you consider a life of sacrifice for the one you have chosen to journey with over the course of your lifetime: *Timing And Intentionality Are Critical.* Notice these important words in Romans 5:6, "For while we were still weak, at the right time, Christ died for the ungodly." Timing and purpose are everything in an environment of self-sacrifice. Too often 'sacrifice' becomes a goal in and of itself, the martyr syndrome. But self-sacrifice must always be couched atop two critical guiding rails: *Timing and Intention.* The death of Jesus occurs along a carefully laid-out plan within the will of God. Jesus is vigilant to ensure it doesn't occur too soon or too late. Hence, Jesus is intentional that His journey to the cross be 'on time'. Always ask the question, "Is the timing right for me to engage in this sacrifice?" The second dimension is equally important to a life of self-sacrifice, "Will this self-sacrifice unleash the optimum circumstances for redemption and healing?" Clearly, both of these dimensions require insight from the Holy Spirit, wisdom from another place, discernment provided by God. Thus, even Jesus paused in the garden, invited His closest allies to pray with Him, asking one more time, "Father, if it be Thy will..." Only when certain of the proper time and place does Jesus help the soldiers up and invite them to come and do what they must (John 18:1-14). And only when the timing is right does Jesus moves intentionally toward His cross.

Over the course of our many years of marriage, we have been offered countless opportunities to sacrifice ourselves for each other and many others. The results were always at risk, never guaranteed. We wish we could tell you the outcomes were all marvelous, skipping through paradise, Candy Land at every turn. But you know better. Life is just too rugged for paradise at every turn. Nonetheless, our lives have been an effort to produce a fragrant aroma for those around us. Live courageously and intentionally for each other, and the aroma around you, and your marriage, will please everyone whose life you touch in the days ahead...

Time for coffee and conversation...

- In what ways have you sacrificed for your spouse?
- Did that sacrifice come with an 'if-then' condition?
- Why is timing and intention so important to the discussion of self-sacrifice?

Action Point...

- Consider one way you could offer your spouse a moment of self-sacrifice.
- Thank your spouse for a moment of self-sacrifice they have offered on your behalf.

> ...gave Himself up for us as a
> fragrant offering and sacrifice to God.
> Ephesians 5:2

" *Love is not a feeling of happiness. Love is a willingness to sacrifice.*

—Michael Novak

Principle 7

Self-sacrifice is the most powerful
transformational force.

Most of us bask in the idea that Jesus died on the cross for us (me). Don't let this ruin your day, but, ultimately, it wasn't about you at all; it was for His Father. No, I don't mean Jesus doesn't love you, but His love for the Father empowers and enhances His love for those things the Father loves (like you). Remember those Sunday School verses from long ago, "For God so loved the world that He gave His only begotten Son..." (John 14). The concept is important. God loves you in the most profound manner, even sacrificing His Son for you, and Jesus loves what the Father loves. Thus, we discover yet another invaluable piece of 'imitation' enabling us to spend a lifetime journeying together: love for God enables you to go to extreme levels of sacrifice for that which God loves (your spouse).

Once again, we stumble onto the particulars of imitating the love of Jesus: *Sacrifice, Even Life Itself, Is A By-Product Of Your Love Of The Father.* This is the essential foundation stone of any marriage relationship. You can do nothing in your marriage more significant than loving God with all of your heart, mind, and soul. Arising out of that love is an incredible desire to love whom and what God loves. It is the unexpected fruit of loving God. Loving God empowers love for others. It is the bedrock of all love.

But let's have a moment of honesty. Few of us engage in sacrifice for the sake of the Father; instead, we willingly, sometimes joyfully, lay down our lives for the ones we love most. The deeper our love for them, the easier it is to sacrifice, to surrender our wants and desires to theirs. But you expect a payoff. We are too pragmatic in our approach. And look out when they payoff doesn't arrive.

I truly, genuinely, with a great deal of hostility crouching at the door of my soul, hate to the make the bed every morning. It's not just a little dislike, I really hate it. It is terribly time-consuming, some days even taking three whole minutes, pushing me to my limits of exhaustion, as I tuck the sheets and covers into the side rails of our bed, knowing full well we are going to mess them up again in 12 hours! Even coffee doesn't help with this cruel, repetitive task! Nonetheless, every morning, while my bride gets ready for work, I make the bed. Why? Because my bride loves a made bed. Thus, a second principle appears: *Loving Your Partner Enables You To Embrace Extreme Levels Of Sacrifice Regarding The Things They Love.* But love for your partner ought not be the foundation of your relationship (yes, I know that sounds odd).

Sooner or later, your incredible spouse is going to fall short of your expectations, fail to meet a genuine or perceived need, or just plain tick you off, as they abandon a trail you expected them to follow. For most of us, it is the inevitable, emotional 'turning point'. In that moment of authentic failure, a 'down the drain' emotional cycle too often begins spinning within your relationship. The cycle spirals downward as your willingness to sacrifice for your spouse begins to diminish with each new disappointment, each missing payoff. Why? Simply because they are no longer worthy of such sacrifice. And with each moment of decreasing desire to sacrifice for your spouse, so the spiral downward intensifies, soon rendering both partners unwilling to sacrifice for an unworthy partner. Thus, the reminder to keep your focus on God the Father and the things God loves (in spite of the brokenness evident to everyone). Loving what God loves, and God loves a bunch of broken and unworthy stuff, especially people, can be utterly exhausting. It may even require imitating the self-sacrifice of Jesus.

After 35 years of counseling married couples, I have discovered very few begin the sessions with, "Let me tell you how wonderful my spouse is…" And if they do, it is typically just the introduction to the unavoidable, "But…" More often than not, they simply begin with the unpleasant list describing the brokenness of their partner. And while the brokenness genuinely needs to be addressed at some point, more important is a review of the fundamental question, "Tell me about your love for God?" I have discovered over these many years, those who have a profound love for God rarely struggle to love in spite of the brokenness of their partners. Loving the people God loves is the unexpected fruit of a vital love relationship with God. God actually pours into us His love, creating in us a love for the things and people God loves. But giving yourself up for the sake of the unworthy is always challenging.

Eventually, everyone asks the same question, "Why self-sacrifice for those so unworthy?" Simply because it is the *most powerful force known to humanity in bringing about authentic heart change in those targeted by self-sacrificial love.* Don't miss the significance of this fundamental truth. Self-sacrifice is the 'Trinitarian method', the way God did it, the way we should do it. But like the effort of Jesus, there is no guaranteed outcome (other than God is always pleased); instead, it is the means by which we release the most powerful relational force at our disposal, thereby creating the optimum circumstances for transformation to occur. But, ultimately, transformation must be initiated by those needing and wanting transformation. Your challenge is to engage in the act of self-sacrifice, thereby freeing a powerful force, the love as God, as you imitate the self-sacrificial love of Jesus. You have an incredible resource at your disposal. The question remains, "Will you unleash it?" Time to mimic His love…

Time for coffee and conversation...

- Why is self-sacrifice so critical in a marriage?
- Do you think you could sacrifice for an unworthy partner?
- Do you really think self-sacrifice is the most powerful relational force?

Action Point...

- Ask your spouse what they deem a 'self-sacrifice' on your part toward them.
- Ask your spouse how you might love them 'self-sacrificially?

CHAPTER 2

The Unexpected Glue: The Art of Sexuality

NOVICES TO THE Christian discussion of marriage often assume sexuality to be a forbidden topic and, sadly, too often it is, as if marriage is designed to thrive in a sexless environment, but nothing could be further from the truth. To the contrary, Paul dedicates a significant portion of Ephesians 5 specifically to the topic of sex, more specifically, sexual immorality. And, wow, does his discussion from 2,000 years ago sound like it was written from the hand of a modern-day prophet; perhaps, an indicator of just how little things have changed over these many years. Sadly, moderns, too familiar with the unexpected by-product of the 'hooking-up' generation (damaged sexuality), often quickly identify with Paul's exhortation to leave all of that (sexual immorality) behind. I hear over and over again from young couples, "We have had enough of all that crap." As one 20-something female suggested to me while I was counseling with her and her husband, "Sex has nothing to do with a good marriage, and I don't care if we ever have sex again." Unfortunately, she is not alone. Tragically, she is greatly mistaken about the God-prescribed role sexuality plays in a healthy marriage relationship.

The unfortunate consequence of too many 'bad' sexual encounters

with young and unexperienced partners is often a less than healthy
view of sexuality and a bag full of insecurities and damaged sexuality.
Understandably so. Sex is an art form, a dance, sometimes an elegant and
peaceful waltz, other times a zesty tango and everything in between. Dance
the wrong dance at the wrong time, in the wrong way, to the wrong tune
and people get hurt, emotionally, physically, and even spiritually. Dance
the right dance and heaven descends on earth, a oneness of another kind,
intimacy bonding in the most potent manner possible. Yes, just like God
designed.

Sexuality done well, really well, provides a dominant bond for any
marriage relationship. It is one of the unexpected relational 'super glues'
God has provided for His children. It is not the only glue, perhaps not
even the best glue, and in some cases, missing all together, but 'super glue'
it is for those who learn to dance well with just the right partner. But like
dance itself, so few couples seem to find the time to dance often enough
to become excellent dance partners. And regardless of your prowess in
days gone by, if you can't glide across the floor with a your life partner,
your gifts are wasted, left behind with dance partners long gone: A tragic
consequence for those who danced their best dance long before finding
their final dance partner.

Another key dimension to a thriving sexual experience is knowing the
difference between 'sex for sex's sake' and 'making love', and all the nuances
in between. Laura and I are often asked, "What is the difference?" In a
general sense, the level of connectivity, the degree of 'oneness' you share
and carry away from the experience. 'Making love' is a comprehensive
experience, uniting two dance partners in a way nothing else can, except
perhaps for tragedy. Sex, on the other hand, while rewarding in its own
way, can only serve as the gateway toward 'making love'. When the two
work in tandem, partners of a special kind, the relationship thrives and
blossoms.

The New Testament deploys three (perhaps four) Greek terms all
translated as love from time to time, yet each with subtle nuances providing

rich insight into the marriage relationship. The best marriages employ all four in their relationship, each adding a much-needed dimension to the marriage experience. *Storgai*, *Eros*, *Phileo* and *Agapé*.

Storgai is often described as the 'old shoe' kind of love. It describes a relationship of warmth and familiarity, comfortable in the best possible way, like those favorite old shoes you just love to wear. Better yet, those old blue jeans no one understands why you still wear. Don goes out of his way to preserve multiple pairs of old, torn jeans. One pair of his worn out jeans has no less than nine patches, each holding those precious, old blue jeans together. Don and I experience this love whenever we slip into bed. He knows within minutes my feet are going to slide over to his side, awaiting their nightly massage from the man who loves me enough to massage my feet each and every night. We then spoon together before drifting off to sleep. No communication needed. After 38 years we just know how it works, without having to think about it. *Storgai* cannot be mandated nor rushed. It can only be coaxed into being as a relationship matures with familiarity and comfort.

Eros (erotic) points to a love rooted in a desire to 'consume'. It tends to be spontaneous and often uncontrollable, rarely paying attention to the directives of the will. Eros frequently drives the early stages of relationships and does so with little regard for the elements necessary for the long haul. Consequently, eros often throws couples together, leaving them in chaos when eros diminishes, as it often does. *Eros,* well suited for initial encounters, a get acquainted period, is poorly suited for choosing mates for a lifetime. While it is an important dimension of most relationships, it rarely sticks around when the inevitable relational stress arrives. Once chaos arrives, eros often departs. It is fickle and undependable unless mastered by skilled lovers.

Phileo is the affection of family, the warmth of relationships united by common blood and interests. Like *storgai*, it arises out of comfortable relationships established over long periods of time, much like family.

Thus, it is often called 'brotherly love', the love of family. *Phileo* rests on common, shared experiences bonding individuals together.

Agapé is typically called 'divine love', reflecting the manner in which Jesus moved toward us, an act of the will, intentionality. It is the love responding to the beckoning of the will. It can be called into action in a moment's notice. It can ignore wrongs, disregard unworthiness, dismiss desires of the flesh to behave differently. *Agapé* responds to the intentions of the human will. *Agapé* is the cherished friend of all who have learned to love well. It is His way of loving.

Sexuality thrives best when all four aspects of 'love' are present. And in the nurturing care of all four loves, sexuality bonds couples together in the most productive manner imaginable. So much more than recreation and procreation, it secures relationships in a surprising and delightful manner. Sexuality is the unexpected relational glue. Those who discover its power and use it over the course of a lifetime will enter into a oneness of relationship like none other.

But among you there must not be even a
hint of sexual immorality...
Ephesians 5:3

"*It is love rather than sexual lust or unbridled sexuality
if, in addition to the need or want involved, there is also
some impulse to give pleasure to the persons thus loved and
not merely to use them for our own selfish pleasure.*
—*Mortimer Adler*

Principle 8

Sexuality is a powerful glue,
bonding couples together in
passionately unexpected ways.

I have discovered, perhaps, because of the deafening silence regarding sexuality in Christian communities, most newlyweds often have a common concern, "What is appropriate in our sexuality as a married couple?" And ignorance, genuine not knowing, once the state of every newlywed couple, has been lost in a land long abandoned in the post-internet era. Today's couples, knowing more than many would like to, enter the sacred ground of sexuality in marriage encumbered by more sexual awareness than any generation before them. Hence, it ought to be expected that many young couples ask the question, "When does our sexuality become inappropriate or sexually immoral?" And that concern is elevated by passages suggesting there must be no immorality within a Christian, sexual relationship. Thus, we have much to discuss over the next few sections.

The term here, *porneia* (the root from which we get porn in English), was typically used to describe sexuality (intercourse, predominantly) occurring outside the code of normative civil or religious guidelines. It was not primarily concerned with the particulars of sexuality but, rather, the setting in which sexuality occurred (within a culturally-acceptable relationship). The question of "What's appropriate?" was left to the individual couple to discern as they stumbled their way through the playground of sexuality. And stumble they did in the proverbial 'backseat of a Chevy' or training ground during the first year of marriage. As you might guess, much has changed since then, but more on that later. Still, why does Paul go to such extremes to insist not even a 'hint' of sexual immorality (sexuality outside the context of marriage) be 'named among you' (the literal translation)? Now, that is the million dollar question.

Some folks have suggested over the years that Paul was simply a prude, unfamiliar with the passions of sexuality, determined to minimize all sexual activity in an effort to distinguish Christianity from the sexually-oriented cults popular in his day. I doubt it. Historically, Pharisees were married, and Paul's insights into marriage seem to arise from well-seasoned experience. I suspect his insights were more along the lines of understanding the profound power of sex, a force far too many developing adults seem to ignore. Sex, even its minimal forms (1st, 2nd and 3rd base as we used to say) is a bonding agent to be reckoned with. Reflect for a moment on that first passionate lover's kiss. Can you still feel the incredible flush of energy, passions literally surging, exploding across every fiber of your being? Remember how incredibly 'connected' you felt with that first encounter? Or, perhaps, yours was a reaction of another kind, unwanted sexuality that left you feeling vulnerable and violated, connected in horribly uncomfortable dimensions. Both are reactions to the bonding mechanism latent in all sexual activity. Once bonded, separation occurs only with varying degrees of unrest and scarring. Who among us has not felt the horrible, emotional pain of initiating a breakup or suffering the angst of being dropped, abandoned, kicked to the curb by that special person who now just wants to be 'friends'. Is there any more painful line, "Let's just be friends." Friendship after sexuality, even for the post-Seinfeld generation, is far trickier than we'd like to admit.

But moderns, caught in the cultural training ground of modern entertainment, seem undeterred in far too many instances. Theirs is a tale of premature sexuality and all the emotional and physical scarring that goes with it. Thinking sexuality could be separated from the emotional bonding prewired into our minds and bodies, moderns put a great deal of effort into learning how to engage sexually without bonding, even naming the effort: *hooking up* or, the even more popular, *friends with benefits.* Unfortunately, it can't be done. My experiences with countless couples over the years has anecdotally suggested no one comes away unscathed in one form or another. Sadly, many couples abandon sexuality in the early stages of their marriage, too traumatized to journey into the outer realms of sexual experience and creativity.

So comes Paul's warning to those who have explored the shores of sexuality prematurely. Leave it behind. It ought not be "named among you." Over these many years, I have discovered too many wounded lovers trying to leave the past behind as they seek to recklessly abandon themselves in the arms of a Godly lover. It is in the arms of a Godly lover that sexuality finds its fulfillment, unleashing a powerful bonding mechanism, perhaps more potent than any glue known to humanity. It is here, surrounded in the safety of a Godly companion, that sexuality finds freedom, vulnerability, and creativity, even for experienced lovers. Once liberated from the scars, wounds, and unrealistic expectations of days gone by, sexuality bonds in ever-increasing dimensions. It is the way God intended, the unexpected glue, uniting couples for a lifetime. Fear not, the pathway toward intimacy of a special kind is still within reach, available to even the most damaged lovers. And for those who have resisted the temptation to explore regions so desirable, incredible days are yet ahead as you recklessly abandon yourself into the arms of your lover...

Time for coffee and conversation...

- Why does God attempt to protect sexuality until it arrives in the safety of marriage?
- To what degree have you mastered the ability to 'hook-up' without bonding?
- Does sexuality still bond you in powerful ways to your spouse?

Action Point...

- Discuss with your spouse the ways you feel safe when engaged sexually.
- Discuss with your spouse the ways you feel vulnerable sexually?

Nor foolish talk, nor crude joking.
Ephesians 5:4

"To love at all is to be vulnerable. Love anything and your heart will be wrung and possibly broken. If you want to make sure of keeping it intact you must give it to no one, not even an animal.

—*C.S. Lewis*

Principle 9

Sexuality creates immense vulnerability, be protective of your lover at all times.

Sexuality exposes you in the most vulnerable ways humanly possible. Every dimension of the encounter removes the normative protective layers of our day-to-day existence, from clothing to emotional shields, it all goes by the bedside. It is in our sexual encounters that we are most susceptible to wounding of the severest kind. Thus, a few ground rules as your journey into sexuality moves forward in an earnest long-term and creative fashion.

Let's start with the basics. You probably are not very good, even if you've had plenty of practice along the way. Lovemaking is an acquired art form, a dance of sorts, always requiring an in-depth knowledge of your partner. And like all art forms, dancing, painting, playing the violin, etc., that knowledge only comes with 'hands-on' experience and no two dancers are ever the same; hence, even experienced dancers struggle to learn the nuances of the same steps with new partners. And yes, much of the sexual journey is about nuances. The better you are at nuances, the better your love dance will be, the stronger the bond.

Prior to the birth of the internet, the best 'experience' most of us could hope for was an abandoned copy of Playboy (a male teenager's prized possession in the 1970s) or maybe some even cruder version of printed pieces of gold. But as most young couples tell me over and over again, those days are long gone. Today's young people have a new kind of experience, the visual canopy of the internet, accessible to almost everyone. Unfortunately, the vast majority of young teenagers (male and female) have been sexually imprinted not in the backseat of a Chevy (my generation), or the hayloft (my Dad's generation), not even the front porch (my Grandfather's generation); rather, they have been ruthlessly exposed to sexuality in the crudest forms possible: *modern porn over the internet.* Unlike previous generations having to stumble their way through sexual experimentation as the norm became boring, this generation is exposed to every conceivable form of sexuality. Nothing is left to the imagination or creativity of the human spirit. The 'blank tablet' has been completely filled in. The remaining questions become: Which forms will you embrace, and how will you use them? How will the two of you choose to dance?

The by-product of sexual exposure of the crudest kind is an unrealistic expectation of what a sexual encounter should look like, feel like, and, most importantly, accomplish when the lust-filled dance draws to a close. Thus, insecurity of all kinds soon develop: *Am I good enough? How do I compare to your previous experiences? Am I meeting your needs?* And on goes the relentless insecurity nagging at most lovers. Hence, Paul's warning to never, not ever, make your sexual ineptitude (or prowess) a source of humor. Humor in the bedroom can too often be a deathblow to intimacy destroying any willingness to engage in the risk-taking of creative sexuality. Sadly, too few couples seem to understand the safety net necessary for creative sexuality and, as a result, unintentionally wound one another in the process.

And rest assured, your encounters, sooner or later, will provide ample material for 'crude joking'. There are just too many opportunities for unintentional chaos in the dance of creative lovers. You name it, chances are it will find its way into your dance of romance. And, sometimes you just have to laugh as you unexpectedly tumble out of bed. But crude humor is never the best response.

Instead, Paul suggests an alternative approach, one of praise and thanksgiving (eucharistia). What an odd place to see the command to praise and offer thanksgiving. Rookies understand the importance of praise and thanksgiving.

When was the last time you truly learned something taking great effort to master? Do you remember? Do you recall the sense of inadequacy as you were trying to get better with each passing day? Conversely, think about the sense of accomplishment surging through you as you mastered the initial elements of a very complicated process? Praise and thanksgiving are a critical part of that learning process. Praise encourages us to move forward, to continue developing, to master the art. Praise is a powerful relational bond, especially in sexuality.

At 19, my (Don) standards for great sex couldn't have been any simpler. Truth be told, I couldn't imagine the concept of bad sex. The two words just didn't seem to go together. Wow, have things changed at 58. I really know what bad sex looks like, especially for my poor bride as she tolerated the learning curve of her young lover. I shudder to think about how many nights in those early days of marriage were great for me (no such thing as a bad night of sex at 19) and less than stellar for my bride. Who knew both of us were supposed to be fully engaged in the sexual encounter and, more importantly, fully satisfied at the end of the erotic dance.

Now years later, we have learned the importance of praise, "Wow, that was delightful!", and thanksgiving, "You are so good to me!" We have discovered a simple truth Paul was pointing out with his admonition to praise rather than deride: *All human beings respond well to being praised and thanked for their efforts!* Conversely, the slightest humiliation will send us scrambling back to the safest places possible. Learn early in your relationship the wonderful art of praise and thanksgiving. It will open the door to sexual creativity. And yes, the dance gets better and better with creativity and experience...

Time for coffee and conversation...

- How has 'imprinting' via the computer screen impacted you? Your spouse?
- Do you think pornography creates unrealistic expectations?
- How do unrealistic expectations pollute the sexual experience of couples?

Action Point...

- Tell your spouse the things they do well sexually and why you enjoy them.
- Cautiously and gently communicate the aspects of sexuality you are not open to.

Instead let there be thanksgiving.
Ephesians 5:4

"*Be thankful for what you have; you'll end up having more. If you concentrate on what you don't have, you will never, ever have enough.*

—Oprah Winfrey

Principle 10

Protect your sexual
imagery of your
partner at all costs.

Learning to be genuinely thankful for your spouse is another learned art filled with slippery nuances requiring volumes of practice. Sadly, far too many people seem to think it comes naturally, the normal response to being with Mr. or Mrs. Fabulous. Rest assured, for most of us, it is not. The 'fabulous' often has a way of rubbing off over the course of the long journey ahead. Learning to keep the luster on 'fabulous' is an important skill for every relationship. Hence, a well-prepared strategy for living with less-than-perfect is necessary.

The confusion often starts in the dating process as thankfulness appears to come naturally during this phase and for good reason. First, your spouse was pretty careful to make sure you saw only the 'good stuff'. Remember the hours of primping for those first dates, the thoughtful approach to just about everything, how you looked, smelled, ate, even your underwear was carefully prepared. Heaven forbid you belch unexpectedly (and a fluffy was instantaneous relational death)! Both of you spent a great deal of energy making sure you put your best foot forward, rightly so. But it was more than just that. You were careful about making sure you either didn't see, or simply ignored, the other stuff. Your good friends saw it, as did your family, even warned you about it. But somehow it alluded you; no, you just ignored it, primarily because you just didn't want to see it, choosing to focus on other aspects instead: the good, pleasing and perfect ones.

Your spouse doesn't suddenly mutate into an alternative creature. That creature was there all along. You simply chose not to see it. And believe it or not, 'not seeing it' isn't a bad approach after all. In fact, it is the foundation of most thriving, long-term relationships.

From the beginning, some aspects of the bathroom have been private, a small piece of our personal space we keep protected. I don't even allow Don to watch me get ready in the morning, things like putting on my make-up or brushing my teeth. It helps me to protect the image he carries of me in his mind. So while we often shower together, there are other aspects of the bathroom we have chosen not to share. We have found there are simply some aspects of married life that do not have to be shared. Some things are better left unknown.

Scripture is filled with admonitions to control our thinking, "Finally brothers and sisters, whatever is true, whatever is honorable, whatever is just, whatever is pure, whatever is lovely, whatever is commendable, if there is any excellence, if anything worth of praise, *think about these things*" (Philippians 4:8). I suspect modern psychology has discovered why the way we think is so crucial to your journey. *Our Feelings Typically (almost always) Trail Behind Our Thoughts.* Hence, learning to control your thinking patterns is essential to the 'feelings' you have toward your spouse. If you think poorly of your spouse, you will feel poorly about your spouse. Conversely, if you think highly of your spouse, you will feel positive. Learning what to think about and how to do it is essential to any marriage relationship. It is vital that we take responsibility for what we allow our minds to think. You are the gatekeeper of your mind.

We have discovered we can choose not to think about some of the experiences we have had over the years. Hence, I really can't remember having many arguments with my husband. Why? Simply because I refuse to think about them. Thus, with each passing day, those memories become harder and harder to access in the memory banks of my mind. Many of them simply disappear over time. But we have also learned an equally or, perhaps, even more important concept: *I Don't Have To Choose Not To Think About Things I Have Not Seen Or Experienced.* Thus, I have never seen my husband in a variety of tasks, ones I would rather not have to think about (keep in mind some of you will think it the coolest thing in the world to be able to share a bathroom. In that case share away!). We call it 'framing', the art of making sure your mind focuses on good *images* regarding your spouse. And framing is an art form essential to any long-term relationship.

Learning to *frame* your spouse in a good light is a foundational skill for healthy relationships. The key is to learn which dimensions to frame and which ones to leave unframed or even unseen. Our TV has a screensaver I love. It loads actual pictures of our family, photos I adore, my all-time favorites, ones we have purposefully and intentionally loaded for that very reason. And each picture appears in an actual frame as it slides across the screen. I smile with each photo, warm, fuzzy feelings floating across my being as each one releases powerful positive images of my family from days gone by.

For the last three decades, Don and I have worked very hard to frame each other only in the best possible light (and there was plenty of bad-light experiences). We purposefully guard our minds, carefully managing the images our minds absorb, refusing to allow negative ones to take root. Conversely, we intentionally 'set our minds' on those things which are good and pleasing. Thus, it should come as no surprise we have equally mastered the art of 'thanksgiving'. And not an artificial 'thanksgiving'; rather, authentic thankfulness as we 'think well' of each other. And our imagery of each other provides a powerful foundation for all sexuality. Guard the imagery gate regarding your spouse. How you picture them in your mind is a powerful tool in your relational toolbox. It may be the most important dimension toward sustaining that relationship with Mr. or Mrs. Fabulous...

Time for coffee and conversation...

- Why is it so important to think well of your spouse?
- What kind of feelings do you have when you think positively of your spouse?
- How do those feelings change if you begin to think poorly?

Action Point...

- Find several pictures you really love of your spouse. Share them with each other.
- Pick 1 or 2 pictures to review daily.

SECTION 4

Let no one deceive you...
Ephesians 5:6

"*My reaction to porno films is as follows: After the first ten minutes, I want to go home and screw. After the first twenty minutes, I never want to screw again as long as I live.*"

—*Erica Jong*

Principle 11

Sexual impurity cripples and corrupts. It is a powerful corrosive in a marriage relationship.

It's a repetitive story I fatigue of hearing, "Without porn, I just can't get there with my wife" or "Why can't I have 'this' in my marriage?", or "Why doesn't my husband want...?", And the list goes on. In the end, Erica Jong summed it up as well as anyone I have ever heard. Let's face it, this is a generation way beyond the first 20 minutes of porn, and, tragically, far too many have simply arrived at "...I never want to screw again." And too many join her evaluation long before the sun sets on sexuality, before the human body calls it quits.

Of course, the sex industry would have you believe a far different tale, one that ends with the best sex of your life, more happily married than ever, all because you learned to spice up your sex life with their help. Here is a spoiler alert: like cigarettes, porn has an initial payoff, 10 minutes of powerful eroticism, but, in the end, *let no one deceive you,* it will strangle every ounce of eroticism you have, and sadly, you may never want to screw again. Yes, like cigarettes, you are addicted before you know what hit you. And the road to recovery is a long, arduous path.

I suppose it goes without saying, nonetheless, few males will arrive on their honeymoon night free from the horrible pollution of sexual impurity. Likewise, things have changed for too many females arriving at their honeymoon suite filled with anxiety concerning what's to come. But their concern is not just for the honeymoon; more importantly, it is a concern for the years ahead. How will we keep sexuality an important dimension of our relationship deep into the journey, even beyond the children, even into the old age that awaits us all? The good news is that it is much easier than the world of porn would have you believe, but only if you are smart enough to embrace Paul's suggestion to avoid (like the plague!) all forms of sexual impurity.

One of the unintended consequences of rampant sexual impurity is the ease of self-satisfaction: *masturbation.* Who could have guessed by the 21st century self-satisfaction would be a primary method for sexuality as porn streams into your private closet? I hear the tales from both men and women over and over again, "It is just way easier to visit my favorite site and take care of myself." Not surprisingly, you just can't build sexual depth and relationship while playing in a private digital playground.

But consider for a moment the 'purposes' of sexuality, and, yes, there are several at the very least. Procreation, making babies, is a no-brainer. But human beings are unique (as far as we know) in finding pleasure in sexuality. When done well, it is one of the most entertaining and pleasurable activities known to the human race; hence, the ease of addiction for those who can't resist the enticing lure of the web. Further, we now know sexuality provides multiple benefits to the human body (reason enough to stay engaged). But, ultimately, sexuality has another critical dimension in every long-term journey: *it is a powerful relational glue.* So much so, it often overrules very intelligent people who know better than to be in relationship. Powerful enough to keep bad marriage relationships in tact. Yes, it is that powerful. I'm always amazed by couples remaining together primarily because of great sex.

I have discovered a common scenario with most of the couples who visit my counseling office. Lots of couples seek help in their marital relationship. Typically, after hearing the initial complaints, I ask a basic question, "Are you here to ask permission to separate (code for "Will God still love me if I leave?"), or are you wanting help to make this lifelong journey work?" My follow-up question is equally revealing, "Tell me about your sexual relationship." I have uncovered an unexpected common denominator among the couples just wanting a little help to make it work: *They have a really good sex life together!* Surprised? You shouldn't be. Sex is a potent relational glue.

Paul reminds us to, "...let no one deceive you with empty words." Sexual impurity is ultimately a corrosive eventually eating away every thread of sexual vitality between a husband and wife. Tragically, once the glue of sexuality is removed, it takes very little in the realm of relationship dysfunction to destroy the bond of marriage. Without the important God-given glue, relationships often crumble quickly. Conversely, those who maintain a vital sexual relationship seem to find enough glue to sustain the journey over life's relational rough patches. Yes, there are always relational rough patches. Thus, it is critical you do everything possible to protect your relationship from the corrosive power of sexual impurity.

Laura and I would love to be able to tell you we never had a moment of relational chaos, but that would be an outright lie (a whopper!). To the contrary, three pretty hellish years. Truth be told, I suspect both of us considered heading to the exit on several occasions. However both resisted, because our relationship is built upon a covenant with God. But it was more than a Godly commitment; we were addicted to sex with each other! Yep, we have always enjoyed the journey in the bedroom. Thus, even in the midst of our roughest relational war zones (and yes, most couples, even the strong ones, have a war zone or two over the course of a lifetime), the sex helped keep us together. Sex is the surprising relational glue sent from the doors of heaven. God created us as sexual beings intending for us to enjoy its incredible benefits throughout the long journey ahead...

Time for coffee and conversation...

- In what ways have you sacrificed for your spouse?
- Why do you think the initial thrill of porn soon goes sour?
- What is the danger of masturbation for married couples? What are the benefits?

Action Point...

- Share with your partner a sexual fantasy you desire to share with them someday.
- Ask your partner how you might fulfill their sexual desires.

...at one time you were darkness,
but now you are light in the Lord.
Ephesians 5:7

"*Sex is properly understood to be not only physical, but spiritual—an ecstatic union of two bodies and two souls, meant to mimic the joy and ecstasy of union with the Divine in Paradise. Two bodies joined together in pleasure. Two souls joined through the connection between two bodies and the wholehearted, enthusiastic, selfless giving of the entire self.*
— Sylvain Reynard, (Gabriel's Inferno)**

Principle 12

Sexuality, reckless self-surrender to another, taps into our deepest essence in ways nothing else can.

A parable is told of the rock climber who, unfortunately, fell from the face of a rock wall, free falling until the safety rope yanked him to a painful sudden stop. Wounded and unable to climb back up, he cried out to God, "Dear God, help me!" In one of those glorious miraculous moments, God answered his plea, "I hear you." Relieved and filled with joy, the wounded climber asked God what he should do. The answer, profoundly simple, came instantly, "Cut the rope." Sadly, the climber starved to death at the end of his safety rope. So goes the unfortunate series of events in the life of many attempting to walk in the 'light' of His ways of being and doing. His ways of sexuality, "...two souls joined through the connection between two bodies and the whole-hearted, enthusiastic, selfless giving of the entire self," requires nothing short of 'cutting the rope', letting go of all the old methods of being and doing within sexuality. And yes, 'cutting the rope' holding you in place for so very long, the rope of self-gratification, is easier said than done; but cut you must if you are to experience the deepest union known to the human experience: divine sexual oneness. The 'light' has come...

'Light' has long been a metaphor for truth and understanding in the Kingdom of God. Conversely, 'darkness' has represented ignorance and a lack of understanding. Paul reminds us of a tragic reality, "...at one time you were darkness" and you lived accordingly, especially regarding your approach toward sexuality. Young and overcome with raging hormones, consumers devour one another, all in the spirit of the age. It is the way of 'darkness' and sadly it wounds and cripples inexperienced and young dancers, often permanently.

The problem, of course, is the value system at play in a 'dark' culture verses a culture of 'light'. The 'dark' culture celebrates consumption (eros), sexuality with personal gratification as the target; hence, the persistent message of the age, "consume whomever you can (but be nice about it if you can)." The end, personal gratification, justifies the means and the unfolding chaos as the culture of sexual consumption devours all comers. The culture of 'light', however, operates with a radically different end in mind. Gone is a reigning concern for personal gratification; instead, a new driving ethic reigns in sexuality: *oneness of the highest kind, "...and the two shall become one"* (Genesis 2:24). And shockingly, for those who dare to walk in the light of divine sexuality, embracing a reckless self-surrendering to the needs and wants of your beloved, an unexpected fruit so desired by the many finally arrives: *oneness more gratifying than mere physical consumption could ever be.* So arrives the 'oneness' of the highest kind, the mimicking of trinitarian togetherness. This is the fulfillment of 'lust' of another kind, the profound desire to be known and to know deeply, to embrace the mystery of oneness, to walk in the light.

The culture of darkness would have you believe no such 'oneness' exists, mere wishful thinking, a myth from the Old Testament, a fairytale for the naive. Robbed of the knowledge of what 'could be', the many surrender the so-called fairytale, content to consume the pleasure of the moment;

unaware of the damage inflicted on the 'oneness' yet ahead for those who walk in the 'light'. And so, the 'darkness' reigns, a sexuality robbed of its mystical power to usher in 'oneness' of the highest kind. Sadly, I too often encounter couples who have never experienced the 'oneness' of two beings becoming one in the mystical encounter of radical self-surrender in sexual union. Content with mere physical union for the moment, theirs is a oneness limited to the physical world of flesh and blood, a fleeting bond, void of the oneness of 'light'. Trapped in 'darkness', sexuality loses its luster, its power to usher those engaged in reckless self-surrender into sexual 'oneness', a merging deeper than mere flesh can allow. Sexuality becomes mundane, an unnecessary remnant of youthful hunger, tarnished and left behind. But darkness is never the last word for those courageous ones who dare to walk in the light of His ways of being and doing. There is always redemption and healing in the 'light'. Hence, the challenge to abandon the darkness and walk in the 'light'.

Marriage is a profound step into the 'light', leaving behind the ways of 'darkness', the culture of 'hooking up'. But it is just that, a mere step into the journey of a lifetime. Nonetheless, it is a significant step into the 'light', a radical commitment to love as He loved, to engage in a life of self-sacrifice, self-surrender, all for the sake of another, your beloved. You will be tempted to cling to the self-gratification 'rope'. Resist. Cut the rope once and for all. Leave the darkness behind and free fall into the life-giving light of God's way. "...and the two shall become one flesh," can only be found in the 'light', His ways of being and doing, sexuality in the 'light'. It is the divine mystery of sexual oneness, entrance into the beginning stages of 'unity' of another kind, a union of essence, the gateway to paradise on earth. But you cannot find the gate while stumbling around in the 'darkness', the old ways of sexuality, the former way of consuming endlessly. This is intimacy in the 'light', sexuality in the light of day, oneness like no other. Time to walk in the light...

Time for coffee and conversation...

- In what ways have you sacrificed for your spouse?
- What do you think 'oneness' in sexuality would feel like, look like?
- What dimension of your sexuality makes you feel closest to your spouse?
- Describe the difference between 'having sex' and 'making love'.

Action Point...

- Describe for your partner your favorite moment of 'oneness' through intimacy together?
- Describe how that 'oneness' made you feel.

...try to discern what is pleasing
Ephesians 5:10

"*We are all born sexual creatures, thank God, but it's a pity so many people despise and crush this natural gift.***

—*Marilyn Monroe*

Principle 13

Try (know) to discern what is pleasing to the Lord and your spouse.

Like all the males of my generation, I knew what my wife wanted in bed; after all, I had talked it over with the guys, each of us well-schooled lettermen from the 'Letters' section of Playboy. We knew it all. And then I got married and tried some of that stuff out with my lovely bride. She was literally stunned at my gargantuan ignorance (keep in mind, I was the educated one of the two!). I suspect the latest generation of males, similarly conversant with each other, well-schooled by the ease of porn on the web, are equally inept in the art of lovemaking. Hence, Paul's further warning, "Try to learn what is pleasing..." How could he have known both genders would be so clueless about each other? Perhaps, more importantly, both so non-committal in genuinely 'pleasing' each other: Consumerism at its very worst.

The decision to *learn what is pleasing* is a critical one. If we were all 'cookie-cutter' models of one another, learning what pleases would be so much easier. But, unfortunately, we are not; instead, human beings are uniquely crafted one-of-a-kind damaged entities. Yep, no two wounded and damaged in quite the same way. Thus, the best we can do for one another is be descriptive (here is what some folks experience) rather than prescriptive (here is what everyone experiences). Everyone must learn what is pleasing not in a generic sense; rather, the specifics of your unique spouse. Specificity matters. Your spouse is one of a kind.

The challenge to start with "*what is pleasing to the Lord*" is a warning for creative and explorative spirits: *just because you can think of it, maybe even enjoy it, doesn't mean it ought to be embraced.* Survey after survey suggests many males secretly embrace the idea of the elusive threesome. But, in the long run, how helpful would that be to your long-term relationship? Hence, the suggestion, "Why don't you run that by the Lord first and see what His take on it may be." Few seem to engage in that safety mechanism, deterred by the misconception, "God hates sexual fun!" Nothing, of course, could be further from the truth. God created sex, even installed a pure pleasure button or two (or fifty!), and wired us to explode with delight when all the right buttons are pushed in all the right ways. And, wow, can you have a pleasure explosion when all the buttons fire on cue. So why the admonition to first "Run it by the Guy upstairs!" In a nutshell, because there are long-term consequences you can't see coming. And God is a long-term thinker.

Several decades ago, when porn was yet in its infancy, a friend dared to share with me a startling reality for he and his wife, "I can't get going if we don't watch porn first." That, of course, was code for, "I'm not even 30, and I am functionally impotent with my wife." Sadly, it is a story I now hear way too often, "I've just lost interest in sex with him/her." Thus, we learn the hard way of God's intent to protect us from the chaos of 'undesirable ways' of sexuality. The issue is not, "God never wants us to have sexual fun!" To the contrary, God provides a format for sexuality that unleashes pleasure in the deepest forms possible, for the longest periods possible. Sexuality is meant to be a long-run game, so much more than just procreation in the early stages of family building. But the run-it-by-God-first suggestion cuts both ways. Countless are the times when one side of a marriage relationship informs me 'this or that particular' is just disgusting and ought never be considered. I always ask the follow-up questions: "Are you sure? Did you run that by God? Did God slam the door on 'that', or were you wounded along the way?" Early in our marriage, Laura commented on how 'open' many of her Christian friends were regarding sexuality. She began to notice the 'openness' came from an unexpected source: *the undamaged gals who had avoided bad sex with young men who didn't have a clue, men primarily driven by raging hormones.* Conversely, gals who had engaged in early sexuality with inexperienced lovers were often guarded and wounded even with their husbands. Let me suggest, some four decades later how often that early observation has played out with countless couples I have counseled. No surprise here. Young males, doped up on raging hormones, make lousy lovers (shocking? I think not), often wounding their lovers.

As Laura and I have journeyed along over these many years, we have discovered a complexing problem: *The Particulars Of Pleasing Constantly Evolve.* The popular business book proclaims, "Who moved my cheese?" Thus, discovering what is 'pleasing' is a constant investigation. In our marriage seminars, I often tell the story from our youthful sex. Laura was determined to ensure her husband never felt the need to sample away from home. So the saying I still laugh at, "Do whatever you want, just don't wake me up!" At 25, maybe even 35, I loved that approach, masturbation in the form of a loving partner. But surprisingly, I began to evolve. My desire to masturbate metaphorically with my bride began to dissipate, eventually almost disappearing completely (cut me some slack here, I'm 58!). Poor Laura. Gone were the days of, "Just don't wake me up." Instead, she was now dealing with a man who wanted a full-blown swinging from the chandelier partner whenever we were together. Discerning what was 'pleasing' took on a whole new meaning for her. No surprise, I now hear from time to time, "I love you dearly, but I am just too tired for a full-blown adventure." Imagine her shock as she now sometimes hears, "Ok, I'm tired too!"

Inevitably, at every seminar we do, somebody asks, "So what is pleasing to God and to my spouse?" I wish we could tell you, give you a prescription, a surefire way to sexual ecstasy. We can't. But here is an idea that often provides a map. Go for a long walk or, perhaps, a quiet dinner and simply ask, "What pleases you?"

Time for coffee and conversation...

- Why do you think our desires change over the years?
- How might you continue to evolve in your sexuality? What does sex is art' suggest?

Action Point...

- On a scale of 1 to 10, share how you would rate yourself as a lover and why.
- Ask your partner how you might be a better lover for them.

Look carefully...making the best use of your time.
Ephesians 5:11

"At the end of your life, you will never regret not having passed one more test, not winning one more verdict or not closing one more deal. You will regret time not spent with a husband, a friend, a child, or a parent. —Barbara Bush

Principle 14

Sexuality is easily strangled by the demands of life. Make the best use of your time.

Life is hectic, more hectic than most of us ever imagined. Work and other adult responsibilities consistently whittle away at the reservoir of time and energy. And while married life does offer reductions in the chaos in some ways, it adds to the mix in others. Hence, most couples struggle to find time for sex, especially the kind of sex initiating the powerful bonding mechanisms God intended. Further, once the children arrive, time and energy become even scarcer in the journey we call marriage. So Paul's challenge to use your time wisely, "...making the best use of your time." And that is never more true than in relationship to sex.

Early in the relationship, time for sex seems to arrive spontaneously; and why not, your hormones are raging and the sexuality playground is now 'legally' open 24 hours a day. Sadly, hormones calm down, the playground seems less enticing, and before you know it, your sexual frequency begins to diminish, sometimes at an alarming rate. More disheartening, perhaps, is not simply the diminishing sexual frequency, but the *lack of desire!* Yikes! That is a serious issue. Unfortunately, sexual desire is a very fragile entity, easily damaged in the rough and tumble world of real life. Therefore, the challenge to 'look carefully' as you march along in a chaotic and busy world. This is an incredibly serious admonition!

After almost four decades of marriage, Don and I have discovered a few really important principles and methodologies we have practiced across the years:

- Prioritize your relationship above all others (including the children): The dating phase seems to unintentionally, without any effort at all, prioritize the relationship between the two of you. Unfortunately, it was not nearly so 'unintentional' as you would like to believe. To the contrary, dating couples go to crazy extremes to win the prize. Add up all the time and energy you put into dating and you would be shocked. This relationship mattered above all things and it showed. The same attitude needs to remain long after the "I do's". Understand the energy needed here is significant and manifests itself away from 'sexuality'. Thus, you will need to find ongoing ways to demonstrate to your spouse they are still the top priority of your life. This single dimension will protect your marriage more than any other factor. Make sure your spouse knows they are always your top concern in life.

- Be Intentional: At some point, you begin to realize, "If we don't get intentional about having sex, it ain't gonna happen until one of us is desperate!" Life just has a way of stealing the time that should belong to sex. Only intentionality will both prevent and steal back some of that time. Get intentional, plan ahead, and know what to expect and when. Are we 'making love', swinging from the chandelier, or just having a 'quickie'?

- Be Spontaneous: I'm not proud of this (I shudder at the thought), but Don and I have been 'caught', literally stumbled onto, more than once in our married life. Those instances all occurred in the midst of spontaneous combustion that got away from us when we were confident nobody was around. We were wrong, multiple times. The private beach that wasn't. The abandoned rest stop that wasn't. The locked door that wasn't. The secluded fishing hole that wasn't. You get the point. Spontaneity often requires a bit of risk-taking, but it sure adds a bit of spice to life!

- <u>Avoid the time bandits</u>: By the time you get ready for work, go to work, get home, make dinner, clean the dish, etc., and finally get in bed again, you are beat, really beat, way too tired for recreational activities. Be prepared to avoid time bandit activities, that while fun, seriously cut into time for better things! TV is a sexuality death trap. Be on the alert for time bandits.

- <u>Prioritize Relationship Getaways/Vacations</u>: The phone call came from Don's folks, changing our lives forever. "You kids need time away to be lovers. Mom and I are coming to get Dustin. We are thinking about taking him to Disneyland for a few days. We will bring him back in a week." Wow, did that transform our marriage. We discovered the 'homeland' just had too many responsibilities to really allow us to relax. But freed from home, we suddenly became energetic young adults again. That transformed our marriage. Not a single year has passed that we don't carefully plan a time away from jobs, kids, and other responsibilities to get reacquainted as grown-ups.

Sexuality, without a doubt, is an unexpected bonding agent in a marriage. But it is not automatic, nor everlasting, without purposeful planning. We have learned over the years how predictable a lack of sexuality is in couples who struggle relationally. Thus, if nothing else, diminishing sexuality is a critical warning sign that more important relational factors are under duress, perhaps, even dying. Smart couples have learned early on to keep sexuality an important part of their relationship. Sex is a God-given relational glue incredibly fun to administer for those who take the time to become the talented lovers God intends...

Time for coffee and conversation...

- In what ways are the demands of life already dulling your sexual desire?
- What day-to-day demands weaken your sexual desire the most?
- What daily routines actually increase your sexual desire?

Action Point...

- Discuss how to make sure sexuality stays alive in your marriage. Develop a plan!
- Describe what you plan to do on a frequent basis to increase your sexual appetite.

CHAPTER 3

The Normal Pattern:

The Art of Mutual Submission

I HAVE DONE MY fair share of marriage ceremonies over these last 35 years. In the early years, the traditional vows thrived (and seem to be making a comeback), repeated endlessly by couple after couple. But no surprise to many of you, modern vows abound, intentionally mindful of avoiding anything even hinting at 'submission'. Instead, modern vows often frolic in promises tied to the nirvana of the dating phase, relational bliss, hormones unhinged. The idea of pragmatic tools for navigating authentic chaos are buried deep in the subconscious. Rarely do modern vows tackle the coming reality of surviving days of conflict the vast majority of couples will face in the mundane decision-making of life (surviving actual relational war is the topic of the next chapter). Pragmatics and useful functionality have been replaced with wishful thinking of undying love, positive emotions, and easy togetherness. Sadly, lofty ideals soon crash on the shores of married life.

Below are just a few samples Google threw at me this morning, as I searched for modern vows:

My One True Love:

I (name), take you (name) to be my (husband/wife), my partner in life and my one true love. I will cherish our union and love you more each day than I did the day before. I will trust you and respect you, laugh with you and cry with you, loving you faithfully through good times and bad, regardless of the obstacles we may face together. I give you my hand, my heart, and my love, from this day forward for as long as we both shall live.

The Man or Woman You Will Become:

I, (name), take you, (name), to be my partner, loving what I know of you, and trusting what I do not yet know. I eagerly anticipate the chance to grow together, getting to know the (man/woman) you will become, and falling in love a little more every day. I promise to love and cherish you through whatever life may bring us.

When Our Love is Simple, and When it is an Effort:

(Name), I love you. You are my best friend. Today I give myself to you in marriage. I promise to encourage and inspire you, to laugh with you, and to comfort you in times of sorrow and struggle. I promise to love you in good times and in bad, when life seems easy and when it seems hard, when our love is simple, and when it is an effort. I promise to cherish you, and to always hold you in highest regard. These things I give to you today, and all the days of our life.

Trust in You Completely:

(Name), with all my love, I take you to be my wife/husband. I will love you through good and the bad, through joy and the sorrow. I will try to be understanding, and to trust in you completely. Together we will face all of life's experiences and share one another's dreams and goals. I promise I will be your equal partner in a loving, honest relationship, for as long as we both shall live.

Only in authentic synergy do two individuals expect to find a harmonious solution to the problems of sustained relationship. And this bliss of the dating phase often suggests the decision-making process will be easy, a merging of two souls anxious to please the other. Nonetheless, it is the long haul that creates the inevitable friction and subsequent drama. Sooner or later, reality sets in, decisions have to be made, and the unavoidable need to 'submit' rises to the surface.

The necessity of submission is the by-product of authentic relationship lived in the confines of real life. Life is the problem. It simply refuses to unfold in a neat and timely manner, a codified approach making all decision-making simple and easy. To the contrary, life is unruly, often uncooperative, frequently flat-out difficult, mandating hard decisions impacting both of you for the rest of your lives. And in spite of all your premarital psychological testing, your practicing by discussing key issues every couple will face, and all the rest, sometimes you will simply see the writing on the wall, an authentic disagreement waiting to happen. Yes, believe it or not, authentic disagreement eventually finds us all. Learning to deal with it constructively is the key to sustaining long-term healthy relationships. Conflict simply cannot be avoided.

Compromise is indeed a necessity for every relationship. Much of the time solutions rise up out of a willingness to compromise, to submit to the wisdom of another human being, most noticeably, your spouse. The two of you are journeying together, because you have learned to trust each other, work together, combine your skill sets in a productive manner. Still, life has a way of forcing you to the limits of compromise. Learning to sustain a willingness to compromise even in the context of radical disagreement is a needed skill set as you journey onward in real life decision-making.

Unfortunately, as you gain insight into the inner workings of your spouse, that willingness to compromise is often surrendered. So comes the need for discovering how to journey onward with a wounded and broken 'other half'. And yes, sooner or later, their brokenness, their woundedness, will rise to the surface, creating in you a hesitancy about surrendering your will to the desires of another.

The temptation to not compromise is the 'devil' in the details awaiting every relationship. Learning to resist the temptation to avoid compromise, and sometimes submission, is critical to the success of every relationship. The pages to follow will offer a few insights into learning the art of compromise and submission.

Have nothing to do with the fruitless deeds of darkness, instead expose them to the light
Ephesians 5:11

"*A painter should begin every canvas with a wash of black, because all things in nature are dark except where exposed by the light.***   —Leonardo da Vinci**

Principle 15
Authentic living is always the best course of action, but only in the safety of permanence.

Perhaps, one of the most challenging dimensions of married life is the slow and arduous revelation of the true self, the damaged and dark self, carefully camouflaged during the dating game. Thus, we have stumbled onto the important first step of normalcy: authentic living. Like it or not, inevitably the darkness reveals itself as close emotional and physical quarters mandate intimacy of a new kind. A healthy marriage relationship enables self-disclosure in ways never possible prior to the assurance of safety and longevity provided by the commitment to a lifelong journey. Safety is essential to authenticity, and it ushers in the opportunity for the wounded self to appear.

For example, consider your approach to all other male/females now roaming the planet. Prior to marriage, you were mildly (ok, strongly) attracted to lots of them. Yes, lots of them. Unfortunately, your marriage commitment did little to dampen that attraction mechanism. Like it or not, the attraction mechanism is still fully operational, a part of your God-given hardwiring and, more than likely, operational for the rest of your married life. No, the commitment to marriage did not kill it, nor will living with your spouse, wonderful as they may be. The attraction mechanism plays a variety of roles in human interaction, many of them helpful and productive over the course of a lifetime. But something has changed. You are no longer on the market. Your card has been punched. Thus, learning to deal wisely with a potentially dangerous operational mechanism in the human psyche is a really an important skill set to acquire. And your spouse can be a key ally.

The problem, of course, is very few of us are initially well skilled at telling the attraction mechanism, "I don't need you anymore in the way I used to, please cease and desist all inappropriate attractions." Instead, we carelessly let the once helpful mechanism continue to operate at half speed thinking, at the proper time, we will shut the mechanism off before it gets out of control. Be warned. This mechanism, once unleashed, rarely pays heed to your pleas. Thus, it becomes essential to learn how to reign the beast in, to use it only in productive ways, rendering it powerless in the old ways of life before marriage. And yes, it can be done.

The secret, of course, is learning to 'expose the darkness', those once healthy dimensions of personhood (no longer helpful or productive) now operating in the shadows, long after their usefulness has disappeared. Early in our marriage, but deep enough in to think we were safe and secure, Laura came home with a staggering confession, "I'm attracted to one of the young men in my class." I remember thinking, "That's not possible, you're married to me, head over heels in love with me, promised for life! Look at the marriage license! This is a sealed deal. You're not allowed to be attracted to another man!" Once I caught my breath, I realized what an incredibly brave step my bride had taken. She was doing precisely what the wisdom of God prescribed, "expose them to the light." In that moment of authenticity, Laura found the courage to 'expose' a risky darkness, a still operational attraction mechanism. Unexpectedly, her courage gave me courage, and I confessed a brewing attraction to a woman I was attending class with at seminary. We were married Christ followers implementing the risky guidelines of God's Word, exposing dark dimensions of our old ways of being and doing. Amazingly, once in the light, once confessed, the attractions died quickly and painlessly.

Light doing exactly what Paul knew it would do, crushing the darkness, rendering it powerless in the light.

Now, here is the important part of this tale. How you react to 'exposed darkness' radically determines the confidence your spouse will have to walk transparently in the days to come. Recoil, ridicule, or wound your spouse, and they will never show you an authentic dark spot again; instead, hiding them far from your critical eye and spirit. Laura and I both responded in love and understanding (not surprising given we were both struggling with the same battle). Consequently, both of us became 'risk-takers' in the days to follow, continuing to expose 'darkness' as it crept into our lives. Some years later, I would confess a momentary succumbing to pornography (back in the day before mail filters and screening). My bride, rather than demeaning me, crippling me with judgement and condemnation, simply loved me, helping me to explore a variety of ways to overcome the 'darkness' encroaching upon my soul, my very being. Rather than 'judge', she became healer and redeemer to my brokenness. And with each self-disclosure of the 'darkness', Laura and I have learned to offer ourselves as redeeming and healing agents in each other's life. We call it, *Learning To Embrace The Dark Side Of Your Lover's Being.* And yes, all of us, everyone of us, have a dark side in need of healing and redemption. Fortunately, God has prepared your spouse to come alongside you, embracing the darkness, soothing the wounds of your damaged inner being.

I am constantly amazed at the 'darkness' lurking in my damaged being some 39 years into marriage. I'm confident Laura experiences those same shutterings. Fortunately, most of the struggles of youth have long disappeared, as Laura and I exposed them to the light of each other's awareness and healing presence. Unfortunately, new shades of darkness have crept out of the shadows. Each of them just as dangerous as the shadows of youth, in spite of their vast differences. Surprisingly, exposing them to the light of day is still tricksy business, a risky endeavor as we risk rejection and further wounding in each other's presence...

Time for coffee and conversation...

- Why is revealing your dark spots such a risky endeavor?
- Why is it so important to pick the right place and time for a moment of revelation?

Action Point...

- Find a simple dark spot you could make known to your spouse.

SECTION 2

Don't be foolish...
Ephesians 5:17

"*There are well-dressed foolish ideas just as there are well-dressed fools.* —Nicholas Chamfort

Principle 16

It only takes a little foolishness to destroy even the best relationships.

Foolishness is seriously frowned upon in the New Testament. So much so, Jesus forbids us from calling one another 'fools', the severest of condemnations, an f-bomb in biblical vernacular. But why? Why does Jesus frown so harshly upon the label, especially when foolish behavior seems in such abundance? To be 'foolish' from a NT perspective is to know what ought to be done, the appropriate course of action, be fully capable of doing it, but still choosing to do otherwise. Moderns would call this being 'unreasonable' (counterproductive), doing something you know is ultimately detrimental to you as a person. That kind of behavior is nothing less than 'foolish'. Unfortunately, a marriage relationship has so little room for foolish behavior. Foolishness is a powerfully destructive tool in any relationship, but especially so in marriage. It simply means you didn't care enough to do otherwise, even when you could have. Hence, the admonition to avoid foolishness whenever possible, instead, learning the 'will of the Lord' (how the Lord would have you to act.)

I have discovered over the years, people are incredibly forgiving toward 'ignorance', an actual lack of data, genuinely not knowing what should be done. And every marriage begins with a lot of ignorance, a lack of data concerning a wide variety of topics regarding 'how' to live successfully with your unique spouse. And, therein, lies the primary challenge: Your spouse is unique, a custom designed one of a kind, who belies far too many of the rules you thought applied to every male/female. Yes, all those prescriptive (do this) self-help marriage books are great for the couple expressing their tricks of the trade, but the problem, of course, is that you are not them! Nor is your spouse exactly like their spouse. Thus, the necessity of acquiring intimate knowledge of the ongoing maintenance needed to keep your unique spouse fully operational over the course of a lifetime. Wow, is that an immense challenge! But with every passing day, your knowledge of your spouse's preferences, even whether the toilet paper should hang over the top or dangling from the backside, will increase dramatically. And with that increase of knowledge concerning the intricacies of your spouse comes the privilege, and sometimes burden, of responding appropriately (their needs above your own).

Conversely and consequently, folks are much less forgiving regarding 'willful' failure, foolish behavior, intentional or careless placement of the 'toilet paper.' But understand, foolishness rarely strikes in full-bloom fashion, all-out idiocy, lunacy worthy of the mental ward. Instead, foolishness strikes incrementally, tiny, seemingly inconsequential steps, more along the lines of drifting. Who really cares which way the toilet paper hangs? Thus, the behavior unfolds typically because the individual has not taken seriously the pending destructive power of foolish behavior over the long haul, the cumulative damage of tiny acts of foolishness quietly gathering in the background. Small steps of foolish behavior often cause minor ripples, barely noticeable in the present moment. Unfortunately, when enough minor ripples collide with a new disturbance in the present moment, the tsunami following is incredibly unpleasant for everyone involved. And heaven help you when the dam eventually breaks, releasing a massive flow of destructive emotional floodwaters stored carefully for months, maybe even years on end.

Don and I have discovered over the years that the 'issue of the moment' is rarely the 'issue'; instead, we are typically dealing with emotional floodwaters that have been building up for quite some time. The issue of the moment is typically no more than the proverbial "straw that broke the camel's back." This is especially true when one of us acts foolishly in the moment. Foolish moments have a tendency to unleash pent-up frustration and angst.

I've learned over the years, it's 'foolish', pure folly, to try and apologize to Don before he is ready to offer forgiveness. When I offer an "I'm sorry" before he is ready, the rage following is often worse than the actual offense of the moment. Sounds illogical, right? Perhaps, but it is the reality of the man with whom I journey and live. It is part of his unique scarring inflicted by the remnants of 'original sin'. Consequently, I have learned to stop being 'foolish', to stop apologizing before Don is ready. The good news is he rarely stays angry more than a few hours. But woe to me if I don't let those hours pass.

Now, here comes the tricksy part in this discussion of 'foolish'. Some folks actually prefer the toilet paper hanging over the top. Amazingly, some folks really like it dangling from the rear. And some folks could care less. But once you discover your spouse has a preference, you now have opportunity to hang the toilet paper in a pleasing manner to your spouse. Over the course of your marriage, you will be stunned at the number of 'things' that actually matter to your spouse. Who would have guessed that my husband really wants me to lay my leg over his while we watch TV in bed? How can that possibly matter? Somehow it does. So I throw my leg over his while we watch TV. Would you believe I can't sleep unless Don holds me in some fashion? How crazy is that? Marriages thrive when knowing and valuing your spouse's preferences, even in the mundane and silly things of life, motivates you to accommodate those desires. To ignore the desires of your spouse is simply 'foolish'. Dare I say that? Resist the temptation to let laziness open the door to foolish behavior. Live wisely in the days ahead. Don't be foolish...

Time for coffee and conversation...

- Why is it critical to know your spouse's preferences?
- How committed are you to honoring your spouse's preferences?
- Do you have preferences that are really insignificant, but still matter to you?

Action Point...

- Ask your spouse what their preference might be regarding the mundane in your life.
- Communicate to your spouse your own preferences.

Understand the will of the Lord...
Ephesians 5:17

"Almost no one is foolish enough to imagine that he automatically deserves great success in any field of activity; yet almost everyone believes that he automatically deserves success in marriage. —Sydney J. Harris

Principle 17

Marriage is a learned art form. Learn early and avoid the pain of ignorance.

The dating process is designed to teach us just how much we have yet to learn about the person we are giving a relational trial run. And most of us figure that out very early in the dating process, quickly slipping into our best behavior mode. Thus, the dating game has a great deal of 'pretense' deep into the game, even till the day of marriage. But once the knot is tied, the lessons authentically begin, and the real game, not the preseason, finally commences. And the faster you learn the difference between the preseason (dating) and the regular season (marriage), the healthier your marriage will be.

Sadly, far too many couples consider marriage the end of the game, rather than the beginning. And, wow, is that a critical mistake. Only in marriage, the day in, day out interaction, does genuine understanding slowly begin to take shape. But understanding who your spouse authentically is still doesn't automatically provide you with a 'how-to' operations manual; instead, it merely provides you with insight into your spouse. Figuring out how to enrich their life is a far tougher challenge. Thus, the need for 'wisdom', the 'how-to' manual for living with and enhancing the life of your spouse.

Learning the 'will of the Lord' (wisdom) is tricksy business. Any average 'Joe' or 'Mary' can learn their ABCs, but learning to spell real words, sequenced in meaningful sentences, strung together in complete paragraphs, part of a story, is incredibly tricksy stuff. Likewise, anyone can learn the ABCs of a healthy marriage (be kind, love unconditionally, satisfy each other sexually, etc.), but weaving the various aspects into a pattern functioning well with your particular spouse, in your unique marriage relationship, is far more difficult. Discovering the specifics needed for your marriage to thrive is nothing less than 'understanding the will of the Lord'. In the end, only the Spirit of God can really provide you with the intimate details of how to best engage life with your partner.

In the early years of our marriage, I was determined to provide my bride with the best possible living conditions. Thus, I set out to completely remodel our 150-year-old home. That was a massive challenge. For years, I spent every available minute tearing out old carpet, knocking down walls, and rebuilding every facet of that house. Laura would feign excitement (unbeknownst to me) over each new accomplishment. But, within days, I was back to the next project, month after month, year after year. Years later, as we arrived in Indianapolis, I commenced again with the complete restoration of our next dilapidated home, an old Stagecoach Inn in desperate need of repairs. Once again, my life was consumed with ripping out the old and replacing it with brand-new sparkling stuff. And once again, Laura feigned excitement for the moment and quickly moved on. But I sensed she really wasn't as enthralled with my efforts as she ought to be. Within minutes, we were in an all-out shouting match, and I was determined to show her just how unappreciated I felt after all this work for her! And then came the words I have never forgotten, "I don't care about your remodeling projects! Why don't you write me a note instead?" I remember thinking, "But women like nests, they are nest builders. How the #*&^ can you not appreciate all the work I have put into this nest?" Yes, somewhere along the line, I read some book proclaiming woman love creating a 'nest' for their families, so I set about helping her create the best nest possible. Similar to the now worn-out line, "All men want is to be respected!" I want a whole lot more than being respected, but that is a story for another day...

Suddenly, I discovered after over 10 years of marriage, I really didn't know my wife at all. I was making assumptions I believed had to be true, had to be valid, had to apply to all women: Nests matter! Perhaps, nests do matter, but not nearly to the degree I thought they did. Wow. Wow. Wow. At least not for Laura. So began my adventure in note-writing to my bride. For years, I made sure I found time to place a handwritten note on my bride's pillow before she got home from work. Imagine, 10 years of my life spent working on projects just to show my bride how much I loved her, and she wasn't hearing "I love you" at all. Instead, what she heard was, "I don't have time for you." Wow. Ten years is long time. And yes, after countless notes, my bride finally whispered in my ear one night, "Let it go, big boy, you don't have to write a love note on my pillow every afternoon." Whew... Who knew writing little love notes everyday would be one of the most exhausting challenges of my life. I gladly surrendered the task. But I have learned how to text!

Thus, the biblical challenge to "understand the will of the Lord." No, not generic principles like 'be nice', 'be kind', and every other 'be..." you can think of. Instead, the challenge is to take all of those generic and important principles provided by God and turn them into working particulars within your marriage. I have learned to weave in a little note-writing, an occasional renovation project, a quiet getaway every so often, a daily text, and the list goes on...

Now, here is the punchline: You can't know the will of the Lord unless you ask. So ask God for wisdom regarding your spouse. Further, you will never really know the will of your spouse, unless you ask, and not just once but over and over again as the years roll on. Hard to believe, but like you, your spouse is always evolving...

Time for coffee and conversation...

- Why do we really need to know the particulars regarding our spouses?
- Why is it so important to frequently ask what your spouse's preferences are as the years roll on?
- What preferences are currently changing in your own life?

Action Point...

- Spend daily time in prayer asking God for wisdom in loving your spouse.
- Spend some time asking your partner what they really need to feel loved.

Do not get drunk on wine...
Ephesians 5:18

"*Always do sober what you said you'd do drunk. That will teach you to keep your mouth shut. —Earnest Hemingway*

Principle 18

Drunkenness is a gateway to incredible amounts of foolish and unwise behavior.

I suspect you have been around a drunk or two over the course of your lifetime. Only on the rarest of days will you stumble onto a pleasant drunk; instead, typically it is an unpleasant experience from start to finish, chaos unleashed, unpleasantries across a broad range of topics. In the course of 35 years of counseling, I have witnessed a reoccurring theme: *drunkenness and marriage rarely (maybe never) mix well.* Thus, Paul's warning to avoid drunkenness.

Perhaps, Earnest Hemingway, a renown drunk in his own day, voiced the problem with drunkenness best in proclaiming, "Always do sober what you said you would do drunk." He was simply pointing to the reality of alcohol's ability to drug the 'gatekeeper of the mind', unleashing verbal foolishness of all kinds. The 'gatekeeper' of the mind plays a critical role in a marriage relationship, holding at bay comments and actions unkind and unbecoming, each reflecting a 'better left unspoken and undone' reality. And yes, there are many dimensions of unwise comments and actions within a marriage often tied to an unpleasant reality in the life of your spouse. Your spouse is not perfect. Sadly, not even close. Thus, you will at times think, "I need a drink!" Resist the temptation. There are better approaches to dealing with a less-than-perfect spouse. Beer goggles rarely solve the problem at hand.

The reality of a less-than-perfect spouse often begins to appear early in a marriage relationship, as the energy required to behave well (a price you were more than willing to pay during the dating phase) dissipates under the wear and tear of life in persistent relationship in the real world. And behaving well, more often than not, requires a conscious effort to overcome our tendency toward laziness. Thus, as you and your spouse journey deeper into marriage, the challenge to do the right thing, from putting your dish in the dishwasher, to making the bed, to eating at the place your spouse loves but you really don't care for, begins to wane, requiring more energy than you are willing to pay. And so, the image your spouse carries of you in their mental picture frame begins to diminish as you surrender to the temptation to take the easy way out, hence, the popularity of alcohol as it offers a getaway from the grind of the real world. And yes, folks have been escaping into alcohol for thousands of years.

But Laura and I have discovered drunkenness is not the only way to drug the gatekeeper. Other agents are equally effective in drugging the 'gatekeeper' and releasing 'better left unsaid and undone'. Anger, lust, love, etc., all have the power to seduce the gatekeeper. Thus, Scripture reminds us to stay sober at all times.

For the most part, I am a fairly decent guy, easy going, not too difficult to be around. More importantly, I have a pretty high tolerance in regards to putting up with what I deem to be nonsense in other people, even from my bride. That is, until I get angry. Once angry, my ability to act sensibly, kindly, disappears in a heartbeat, unleashing a torrent of 'should have left unsaid or undone' creating chaos, often with unpleasant consequences for months to come. I often refer to these moments as 'out-of-body experiences', as my conscious and 'in-control self' is captured by the anger raging in me, sometimes holding me prisoner for hours on end (see Paul's description of this madness in Romans 7:15ff as he describes doing things he hates to do). The principle Paul points to regarding drunkenness is very simply: *Avoid Being Out Of Control At All Times.* Those who lose control often discover the pain and chaos unleashed by the out-of-control self.

With that in mind, let us suggest several alternatives to the 'out-of-control self' often looming just around the corner.

Resist the temptation to surrender to relational laziness: Alcohol, so I'm told by those who drink socially, is nothing more than a legal relaxer, a way to step out of the wear and tear of day-to-day living into a world of peace, a place where stress seems to just evaporate into midair. Even though I personally refrain from alcohol, I certainly get it. Hiking across the Grand Canyon provides me with the same glorious sense of well-being. Nonetheless, resist the temptation to find that place of rest until the relational hard work has been done for the day.

Deal with the minor issues long before they have time to become major issues: Several months ago, I read a piece on social media by a man who titled the article something along the lines of: "My Wife Left Me Because I Didn't Put My Dishes In Dishwasher." And no, that's not why she left him. He goes on to explain the message behind not putting the dishes in the dishwasher. In a nutshell, his bride heard with every dirty dish left in the sink, "I don't care enough about you to put this dirty dish where I know you think it should go." Do the smart thing, put your 'dirty dishes' in the dishwasher before the pile of minors becomes one big major threatening your marriage relationship.

Learn to identify 'gatekeeper slayers' and avoid them at all cost: Rolling into my 59th year of life, I have discovered a good number of 'gatekeeper slayers'. Insignificant in my life when I keep them at bay, highly destructive when I don't. Top of my list: Get enough sleep on a daily basis. Amazing how much easier life is when I am well rested. Secondly, don't get angry. Once I hit anger mode, look out. Learn to identify your 'gatekeeper slayers', and keep them a safe distance away from your marriage.

Time for coffee and conversation...

- Why do we need to stay sober at all times in a marriage relationship?
- Why is it so crucial to keep the 'gatekeeper slayers' at bay?
- What guidelines might you use to keep the 'gatekeeper slayers' under control?

Action Point...

- Identify your 'gatekeeper slayers' and share them with your spouse.
- Discuss with your spouse how to keep the 'gatekeeper slayers' at bay.

Instead, be filled with the Spirit...
Ephesians 5:18

"*I'm married. I have three children. I have a mortgage to pay. The plumbing breaks and the yard needs trimming. However, what my wife and children need most from me is my passion for them.* —John Eldredge*

Principle 19

Sustaining a passionate love affair requires more than human effort. Such love can only be found in the infilling power of the Holy Spirit.

Sooner or later, most couples realize the challenge ahead: sustaining a passionate relationship over over the course of a lifetime, the grand prize of human relationships, is a mammoth task far exceeding the norms of human relationships. Sadly, I suspect the vast majority of couples settle for something less, a marriage lacking the zeal and passion God intended for married life; instead, too often settling for friendship, living companions, comfortable old shoe relationships. And while finding a great 'roommate' for a lifetime is a wonderful accomplishment, it is rarely the 'grand prize' most newlyweds seek. But there is another level, a passionate love affair transcending the wear and tear of the day-to-day grind. Achieving the ultimate goal requires assistance beyond the norm of human relationship. So the call to be filled with the Spirit in your quest for the 'grand prize' of human relationships.

Nonetheless, at some point, most couples begin to realize hormones wear off, relational techniques aren't quite enough, and communication just doesn't get it done. Life has a way of 'beating us up' as the pressure to pay the mortgage, feed the kids, take the car to the shop, wash clothes, vacuum the floor, and the list goes on and on. For most of us, the cauldron of life seems to intensify with each passing day. Time and energy easily spent on your partner during those early days of dating are soon gobbled up by the demands of life. Tragically, by the time you find time to bask in the presence of your favorite person on the planet, you are exhausted, worn out, incapable of providing your partner with the relational and physical 'prime time' they deserve. And the feeling is typically mutual, both of you simply too exhausted to provide, or even desire, the 'prime time' necessary for a thriving relationship deep into the journey of marriage. Thus, on goes the TV as the resulting relational coma creeps toward even the nicest of couples. And when the relational coma finally arrives, so too comes an impending moment of terrifying awareness. You wake up, TV entertaining no one as it yaks into the night. Startled, drool running down your chin, out of the corner of your eye you notice your spouse, equally comatose, the tragic destiny of every exhausted couple, the relational coma in all its glory. And then you say it, those terrifying words, the climactic moment of despair and horror, "Oh my God, it's happened, we've become like everyone else, more interested in TV and a good night's sleep than we are each other! Aghhhhhhh!!!!" Too depleted to engage, you surrender into the arms of the relational coma, content to slumber quietly with your drool buddy. And so, the journey into average earnestly begins...

Some couples, understanding the value of the 'grand prize', refuse to surrender to the relational coma, wisely engaging every skill set known to humanity. They will spend a great deal of energy and time learning communication skills, relationship skills, parenting skills, money management skills, sexuality skills, etc. And wisely so. These are the foundational tools every couple will need as they journey through a lifetime of ever-changing circumstances. Still, as the grind of life whittles away, even these skill sets will not keep the relational coma at bay. Thus, God offers a Plan B for the wisest of couples as they rise from the ashes of the mundane, move away from the flickering electronic screen...

The mundane inevitably leads to despair, and out of despair a new understanding begins to appear over the horizon: *expert techniques are not enough to create nor sustain the grand prize of human relationships.* The 'grand prize', only available to the most disciplined marriage participants, requires an energy and zeal far beyond the abilities of even the best marriages. With a new understanding regarding the intricacies of marriage comes the awareness a third party is needed: The Holy Spirit. Many aspects the best marriage has to offer simply cannot occur without the infilling and empowering of the Holy Spirit. Forgiveness, Submission, Self-Surrender, Sacrifice, etc., are powerful character traits. These advanced traits, super-gifts if you will, are the byproduct of the infilling of the Holy Spirit, God's provision for the most challenging aspects of marriage. Only the Spirit can consistently empower the super-gifts into fully operational mode.

Without the empowering of God's Spirit, any and every difficult discipline of married life will drain the vitality and enthusiasm out of each act of sacrificial love. Conversely, if empowered by the life-giving presence of the Holy Spirit, sacrificial love will produce zeal and gusto as you bask in the ability to actually 'be and do' in the ways of the Serving King. Like a child learning to walk, this newfound power and zeal requires practice and consistency, unleashing a profound relational tool into your relationship: passion for your spouse (and eventual children). Passion is a delicate flower requiring the nurturing presence of the Holy Spirit. Resist the temptation to buy the cultural lie, the expectation that passion will die with familiarity. In the power of the Spirit, passion thrives and blossoms across the decades. It, too, is an unexpected fruit of life in the Spirit. Imagine the possibilities of a marriage filled with passion and zeal across the decades. Only life in the Spirit can provide the needed vitality for a lifelong journey in a passionate relationship. Find your way to the Spirit and embrace life to the fullest...

Time for coffee and conversation...

- Why is it critical to be empowered by the Holy Spirit?
- Why might we call some gifts the 'super-gifts'?
- Can you identify any 'super-gifts' in your own life? Your spouses life?

Action Point...

- Discuss with your spouse how you might engage a relationship with the Holy Spirit.
- Discuss those aspects of married life you have discovered require the Spirit?

Singing Praise...
Ephesians 5:19-20

"*I praise loudly. I blame softly.* —*Catherine The Great*

Principle 20

Marriage ought to be a shower of praise and thanksgiving to and for your spouse.

Several decades ago, Garth Brooks released a song I enthusiastically sang driving down the road, *Papa Loved Mama*. The song tells the story of a truck driver whose bride was unfaithful while he was on the road. One day he comes home early only to discover his bride is being unfaithful at the local motel. The refrain as he drove his truck into the motel room still rings in my head, still makes me grin (I will get in trouble just for mentioning this), *"Well the picture in the paper showed the scene real well. Papa's rig was buried in the local motel. The desk clerk said he saw it all real clear. He never hit the brakes and he was shifting gears!"* My bride did not find it amusing, and the tune was soon banished to the 'no play' zone. Seriously, she did not see the humor.

The principle is called "framing" and points to the importance of 'framing' or thinking about your spouse in the best possible light. Laura's frustration with my continual singing of that little ditty was the repetitive message it bore into my brain, "She will cheat, get ready to shift gears as you drive your rig into the local motel." Understandably, that was not a message she wanted blaring into my mind day after day, as I sang along with Garth. There are much better images to repeatedly imprint on your mind regarding your spouse.

It was a principle I would teach to my teenage son a decade later, as I challenged him to genuinely listen to the typical music of his youth. We hopped into his jeep and popped in his favorite CDs (does that tell you how long ago this was!) and inventoried the messages of the songs he loved. Over and over again, women were demeaned, made out to be sex toys, called vulgar names, etc. After listening for some length of time, I finally asked him, "Would you marry one of the girls you sing about so enthusiastically? And if you did, would you treat her like your music suggests, call her vulgar names..." His response, "Hell no! I just like the music and it's fun to sing." I have continued to shake my head in amazement across the decades, as I hear the music people listen to, sing along with, as if the repetitive nature of the song has little or no impact on the emotional condition of the mind.

Few of us seem to take seriously the unconscious and yet persuasive nature of music as a powerful tool pulling on the mind, teaching it how to think, to feel, and, perhaps, even to act. I'm always irritated when a song captures my mind. You know the drill, endless playing in your head as you bemoan, "I can't get this song out of my head." Hence, Paul's warning to be careful what you sing, "Sing praises." It is a reminder to protect your mind against the persuasive power of negative messages in music.

Conversely, I have a collection of songs I call the 'Laura Collection'. Most of them are from the days of my youth, Billy Joel, Chicago, ZZ Top, and even a Beyoncé tune, and the list goes on. Admittedly, each of those artists probably sang songs that would flunk my 'sing well' criteria, so don't take this as a blanket endorsement. But my collection is made up of songs reminding me of the woman I love. I play them whenever I run, hike, or cruise down the highway by myself.

In so many ways, Laura and I couldn't be more diverse. She loves to dress up, is calm and quiet most of the time, avoids chaos at all costs, really enjoys the finer things of life, and could live at the mall if she really had the money to shop at will. I, on the other hand, love old blue jeans and t-shirts, the outdoors, taking risks of all kinds, any kind of adventure you can throw my way, and would rather go to the dentist than go shopping. It was pretty obvious right from the get-go we were the proverbial opposites that attract.

Those realities became clearer and clearer as we crossed five years of marriage. In 1983, Billy Joel released a song that would soon become a major hit, and I have sung it for decades, still reminding me of the incredible woman I call my wife. Here are a few lines from the lyrics:

I'm gonna try for an uptown girl, She's been living in her white bread world, As long as anyone with hot blood can, And now she's looking for a downtown man, That's what I am...

And when she knows what, She wants from her time And when she wakes up, And makes up her mind, She'll see I'm not so tough, Just because, I'm in love with an uptown girl, You know I've seen her in her uptown world, She's getting tired of her high class toys, And all her presents from her uptown boys, She's got a choice...

Uptown girl, You know I can't afford to buy her pearls But maybe someday when my ship comes in She'll understand what kind of guy I've been, And then I'll win...

Thus, I practice the art of 'singing praises' regarding the woman I adore. No more Garth Brook songs about driving into the local motel. Instead, songs reminding me of just how incredible my bride really is. I really do have the 'Laura Collection', and I play them loud and often.

Like Catherine the Great, Laura and I have equally learned the importance of being critical in our 'softest' voice. Rarely do we engage in critique of each other. That job is left to good friends who gently remind us of our many shortcomings. Thus, we both have good friends who journey with us, calling us out when needed, encouraging us to do better even in the midst of critique. But when it comes to one another, praise is our favorite song, and we sing it loudly and often...

Time for coffee and conversation...

- Why is it so important to constantly think well, sing well, regarding your spouse?
- What songs make you think of your spouse and why?

Action Point...

- Share your 'spouse collection' with your spouse. Tell them why each song made the list.
- Spend some fun time discussing the lyrics of your favorite songs in the collection.

Submit to one another out of reverence for Christ.
Ephesians 5:21

"Rightful liberty is unobstructed action according to our will within limits drawn around us by the equal rights of others. I do not add 'within the limits of the law' because law is often but the tyrant's will, and always so when it violates the rights of the individual. —*Thomas Jefferson*

Principle 21

Radical equality demands nothing less than equal radical submission one to another.

Few, if any, relationships have radical equality; instead, one or the other holds the upper hand, even if just by the tiniest of margins. As the old saying goes, "Power is in the hands of him/her who loves the least." Thus, the one who loves the most often surrenders to the will of the one who loves the least. Further, the weaker almost always submits to the will of the stronger and, too often, only after a tragic and painful battle. Only in the Trinity, the Godhead, do we find radical equality, true evenness on every front, homogeneity across the gamut of dimensions representing what it means to be God. The Trinity is the only community of authentic, relational equality in every dimension of being; equal love, equal abilities and experiences, equal wisdom and insight. Consequently, only in the Trinity do we discover a blueprint for mutual submission, enabling beings of extreme equality to live in harmony and peace, even when they differ on the appropriate course of action, "Nevertheless, not My will, but Yours be done" (Luke 22:42). Incredibly, Jesus surrenders to the will of the Father, even in the most difficult moments of His life, horrible consequences ahead.

Unlike the three persons of the Godhead, Father, Son, and Holy

Spirit, marriage never unites two individuals with *authentic, radical equality*; instead, more times than not, it unites two very *unequal parties*, each with unique gifts and strengths surrounded by a multiplicity of weaknesses and glitches. Sensing a void, human beings are often drawn to another human being equipped with gifts and graces they lack. So the old saying, "Opposites attract." And when they do, marriage is frequently their destination.

The resulting problem, people gifted and yet wounded in different ways, often struggle to surrender to the leadership of another, even when surrendering an area of weakness to a strength area of their partner. Conflicts of 'will' soon manifest in those linked in marriage, if not sooner, then later.

Most couples quickly realize the strengths of their spouse and surrender with little struggle to the profound wisdom of letting the more gifted partner lead when appropriate for any given area of weakness. For example, Laura is a gifted 'people reader'. Almost within minutes of meeting a person, she can quickly discern moods, insecurities, motives, etc. I am constantly amazed at how right she is most of the time. Conversely, I can't read a person even when they wear a sign proclaiming, "I'm a no good bum, stay clear!" Countless times in our journey together, Laura has cautioned me regarding this or that individual, and I have ignored her warning. Chaos typically follows. And sooner or later, I hear those words I dread, "I told you so."

Thus, God's Word challenges us, "Submit to one another out of reverence for Christ." It is the simple recognition of a profound lack of 'radical equality' in the particulars for most couples. More often than not, the skill set of one marriage partner will outweigh the other's in any particular arena, and vice versa. In our marriage, anything relating to 'details', those annoying specifics needed for life's journey, are the domain of Laura. I'm just not a detail guy. Conversely, Laura is a cautious decision-maker. She has learned to trust me when a quick decision is needed. Who leads in our relationship changes like the wind, from moment to moment, circumstance to circumstance.

Perhaps, more problematic for most couples is the arrival of a dilemma for which each partner is equally well suited, but, they arrive at different solutions to the problem. Hence, smart couples soon determine, "Is this worth fighting for?" and the answer in a majority of instances is of course not. One or the other surrenders with little fanfare. It's just not worth the fight.

Eventually, most marriages hit that critical moment, an issue finally arriving deemed worthy of a fight by both parties. Neither willing to surrender quietly. Chaos typically follows, if not all-out war. Sociologists, and those who study marriage relationships, often suggest the battle zone revolves around a handful of issues, inclusive of, but not limited to, the following: Finances, Discipline of Children, Sex and Careers.

Wise couples soon learn the art of surrendering to the insights of another in times of radical disagreement. Laura and I have found a mediator is often an easy solution. We agree to trust the leadership of a third party with little or no vested interest in our dilemma. Those playing the role of mediator have varied over the years. Sometimes a family member, friend, or a counselor. During one of our most difficult seasons of life, we needed a decision regarding how to approach our oldest son. His life was in mayhem, we were both too invested to see clearly, and the resulting unrest threatened our ability to find a 'common ground' approach to our son. In that moment of chaos, I sought out a trusted counselor and friend who provided a solution allowing both of us to step out of the decision-making role. Neither of us were thrilled with the direction he sent us, but both realizing our lack of emotional balance made it essential to trust the wisdom of another. Learning to submit to the each other and, on rare occasions, someone else is a critical skill for every marriage relationship...

Time for coffee and conversation...

- Why is it so important to know who should lead and when?
- What areas would you say your partner is better suited to lead?

Action Point...

- Share with your spouse the arenas of life they are best suited to lead.
- Share with your spouse the arenas of life you think you are best suited to lead.

CHAPTER 4

❧

Conflict Resolution: The Art of War

The myth continues to thrive deep into the modern era: *Communication will always bring harmony.* Unfortunately, the myth thrives because human beings are resistant to the reality of differing opinions. Thus, learning to cope with authentic disagreement is an underdeveloped skill in almost every human relationship. Some offer the often heard attempt, "Let's just agree to disagree," but rarely do those uttering the phrase seek to remain in authentic relationship. Instead, such words are offered as a means of exiting the relationship peacefully, or creating enough relational distance the 'cause of offense' doesn't have to be dealt with on a day-to-day basis. But as you might imagine, marriage rarely offers a comfortable buffer zone; instead, it mandates the 'cause of offense' to be navigated on a fairly consistent basis, sometimes even daily.

As noted in the previous chapter, 'mutual submission' is the norm within a healthy marriage relationship. Typically most couples find a working balance as each partner takes a turn at submitting, more times than not, simply because the issue is not worth fighting over, or the other person is a much better decision-maker regarding the area of concern. Almost seamlessly, couples learn to surrender the lead at the appropriate moment, and just as easily step back into the role of leader at the necessary time. But what happens when a 'worth fighting over' issue arrives? That is, you disagree and think the issue is worth the ensuing battle. Many studies seem to suggest the death of a marriage relationship centers around a surprisingly short list of such topics: *finances, sexuality, careers, and children*. Tragically, once activated, the hot topics infect across a broad spectrum of 'not worth the fight' issues. And war, once engaged, even over trivial matters, is amazingly contagious. Thus, battle lines are typically formed over a short list of concerns deemed worthy of the fight. But once you have stumbled onto one of the 'worth a fight' topics, your marriage enters into a very precarious zone as the infection spreads like wildfire, consuming the relationship in its heated storm.

Far too often, the war zone, those areas deemed worthy of a fight, create a deadly relational atmosphere. The ensuing battles seem to rage endlessly as each partner battles for supremacy, convinced of their 'rightness' regarding the cause of battle. Even worse, the battle mode often drifts into a good number of issues not 'worth fighting over'. Soon battles erupt across the marriage landscape, even over the frivolous matters of life, the infection raging out of control, poisoning far too many aspects of life for the marriage to survive. The relationship soon becomes an endless battle zone. Unfortunately, once in this land of battle, many marriages simply experience a fight to the death, ultimately ending in divorce and the tragic loss of the marriage. And the pattern tends to repeat itself in all future relationships, manifesting over and over again as those engaging never learn to war properly. Hence, the need to find a new way of relating, one saving the marriage relationship as it is employed at the original point of conflict. Too few couples seem to find this elusive way of 'being and doing', the way of the Trinity, instead, thinking submission in the midst of radical equality only an illusion. Rest assured, there is another way, a way modeled for us in the 'radical equality' of the Trinity.

Our conversation began with the discussion of 'radical equality' as modeled within the theological discussion of the Trinity. By way of reminder, 'radical equality' suggests the three beings of the Trinity are uniquely equal, radically equal, and functionally equal across the board. But their equality and 'oneness' does not produce unilateral like-mindedness. Consider the pivotal point of history, the crucifixion of Jesus, the supreme example of harmony in the midst of authentic 'unlike-mindedness'. Hours before the event is to unfold, Jesus approaches God the Father with a question, "My Father, if it is possible, let this cup pass from Me, nevertheless, not as I will, but as You will" (Matthew 26:39). Notice the difference of 'will' between the Father and the Son. Jesus hints at the possibility of another way, a way different from the plan of the Father, His way. Two radically equal beings caught in the momentary dilemma of divergent wills, differing ways of being and doing. But it appears the persons of the Trinity have a predetermined method regarding conflict management, an approach providing direction in those rare moments of 'worth fighting over' issues, a way of 'being and doing' determined long before the moment of crisis actually appears.

Over 30 years ago, I sat in a room full of ordained elders (preachers) in the Church of the Nazarene. I sat in a lone chair facing a long table full of individuals assigned with the task of determining whether or not I should join the ranks of the ordained. I knew all the men and woman in the room having served with most of them for many years. But the atmosphere was solemn, a final interview before being approved for ordination.

Then came the first probing question, "What is the role of the Father in the Trinity?" Every eye turned toward me as silence filled the room. I sat there for a moment, thinking about the appropriate answer, scrambling, knowing I had never been asked that question in all the previous exams I had faced over the last decade of preparation for ordination. Finally, with a bit of trepidation, I gave it my best shot, "The role of the Father is to set the limits and parameters of that which the Son and Spirit will do." The room was uneasily dead silent for a full 10 seconds, seasoned pastors seriously considering what I had offered. Then, without a noticeable cue, the entire group broke into howling laughter. I confess, I sat there bewildered and clueless. Finally, as the laughter softened, the leader of the group clued me in as he turned to the man on his left and suggested, "I told you he would try to answer that one!," and the group erupted into laughter once again. My interview was over. I made it in.

Still, without even realizing it, I had stumbled onto a topic that would guide my approach to marriage for the decades to follow: *Functional submission amongst radical equals*. Over the last 30-plus years, I have performed more marriages than I can remember. Each of those ceremonies has celebrated the call to embrace biblical principles amongst radical equals, husband and wife. If you have made it this far, hang in there and finish the next seven sections discussing the principles of Ephesians 5. You will be tempted to turn and run, to ignore the difficult challenge to mimic Christ in the days of authentic disagreement. But for those who hang in there, those who wade through the challenging pages to follow, a pathway will soon become clear. And those who stay the course will discover an incredibly unintuitive approach to marital bliss, a path through the thorny issues of married life, even those moments of profound disagreement.

In the following pages, you will explore the most difficult, and yet rewarding, stages of the marital relationship: *Survival techniques in the 'worth fighting for' zone*. First, a quick examination of submission in general, a military concept essential to survival in time of war (unnecessary in the normative peaceful days of marital bliss). Second, an examination of the specific roles determined by God for those deeply engaged in marital conflict, even all-out war. And no, the role of husband and wife are not alike; rather, they are unique, challenging, and pragmatic, enabling survival in the most difficult stages of marital warfare. Rare will be the days when these survival techniques will be necessary (we have used them less than a dozen times in our marriage), but when they are, be prepared to mimic the ways of the Trinity. Only in their ways of 'being and doing' can you find the needed resources to survive the art of war.

Mutual submission is the normative pattern for marriage and a multitude of relationships across the spectrum of life. When the principles of submission are operating as God intended, bathed in humility, love, and graciousness, they become invisible, holding relationships together, especially in the life of the community of faith. This unity goes unnoticed by others who assume a natural cohesion, rather than the unifying presence of the Holy Spirit in the midst of authentic disagreement. Thus, give careful consideration to the sections to follow. Successful submission brings life and vitality. An inability to submit will ultimately usher in chaos leading to the death of a marriage relationship. But those who learn to mimic Godly submission within the Trinity soon discover an intimacy and joy only the very few seem to embrace. It is the Divine way of 'being and doing', the key principles for those ready to embrace the final stages of paradise.

War Zone Ahead:
Proceed With Caution

Submit to your own husband as to the Lord...
Ephesians 5:22

"*True strength lies in submission which permits one to dedicate his life, through devotion, to something beyond himself.***

—*Henry Miller*

Principle 22

Crisis scenarios
require out-of-the-norm
solutions rooted
in authority.

In most English translations, Ephesians 5:21 is set off from the section on marriage. The separation creates a tragic mistake, setting the stage for massive misunderstanding regarding the biblical concept of functional mutual submission within radical trinitarian equality. Further, when the guideline of mutual submission is abandoned, the resulting submission too often becomes nothing less than modern slavery under the guise of a patriarchal Biblical worldview. Nonetheless, the entirety of Paul's inspired thought rests upon the reality of 'submission' as a form of life from infancy onward, a practical reality appearing in a broad spectrum of issues from work to the playground. Learning to submit in life, whether to a parent, boss, or coach, prepares one for submission in marriage at the appropriate moments within every healthy marriage relationship. And submission is an integral part of every healthy relationship.

The Biblical concept of submission (*hupotasso*), the same term used in Ephesians 5:21 regarding mutual submission, is an interesting choice by the Apostle Paul. The term is a military term rooted in the practical realities of war. No army can survive following orders from different leaders whose opinions on battle plans may differ. And yes, there are lots of ways to approach every problem in life, war, and even marriage; hence, the necessity of deciding who will call the shots in times of crisis. The act of submission is a pragmatic approach to authority flowing in a top down manner. Like the military, any authority one has is an authority passed down the line from person-to-person.

Thus, submission is rooted in the idea of transferred 'authority' rather than superiority. This is a crucial distinction, extremely important for you to grasp if you are to understand how submission works, especially in a marriage. It is not about who may or may not be superior in any particular aspect; rather, it is a concept utilizing a line of authority established by one who has the authority, via actual superiority (Jesus), to establish any and all lines of authority within human relationships. For those in the church, that person is quite naturally, Christ Himself.

This principle is particularly important for those in a marriage relationship, precisely because there is often a lack of authentic superiority in either partner. That is to say, one partner is not superior to the other; rather, they are equals who must find a way to navigate through life and marriage in an efficient and pragmatic manner when genuine disagreements arise. When couples forget this principle, they often engage in a battle to establish superiority in the relationship and often fatally wound the marriage in an effort to demonstrate superiority. The interesting aspect of the term Paul uses, and its function in the military, is that even if superiority could be established in a particular area, that would not overrule the line of authority previously established. The one who may be superior must still submit to the one who has received the transferred authority.

Those who marry enter into a line of authority independent of actual or perceived superiority; instead, embracing a relational line of authority established by God. However, let me remind you here, every good leader knows when the best thing to do is to ask someone under his/her authority to lead in a particular situation. Yet again, the line of authority stays in tact whether that leader has the common sense to deploy the talents of someone under their authority or not.

The military system of authority is pragmatically efficient, because everyone is operating on the same principles. There is no debate about whom the leader is or whether or not the leader's decisions are going to be followed. Decisions are followed, good, bad, or indifferent. In military scenarios it's easy to see why quick rules of authority are necessary for survival. Time will not be wasted arguing about who would be best suited to lead in this particular situation; instead, the line of authority has been established, and everyone has agreed to follow it. It is the military way. Submission to authority is an extremely efficient system.

In the marriage scenario, the leader establishing the line of authority is no less than Christ Himself. Hence, Paul is reminding believers the lines of authority have been established by God and flow downward in all of life's relationships. Even in the life of Christ, the model of submission is demonstrated. Believers ought to recognize Christ as the General establishing and authenticating the line of authority in the life of the church and even marriage. When submitting in life and marriage, particularly when you suspect your opinion is superior, crucial to remember you are actually submitting to the superior will and mind of Christ, who is overseeing the whole process. As you will see in later sections, this is extremely important for the marriage relationship where some people will assume more leadership than they ought.

Further, the submission of which Paul speaks is rooted in a relationship with God through which the Holy Spirit empowers the believer to do what otherwise might be undoable (surrendering to policy or action you find inappropriate). The real motivation for submission is one's relationship with the Holy Spirit as He empowers. I would suggest to you it will take an infilling of the Holy Spirit to mimic the behavior of Christ in submitting to your husband in times of radical disagreement...

Time for coffee and conversation...

- Why is it important to understand authority as 'passed down'?
- Do you see the value of not having a battle over who is superior?

Action Point...

- Discuss how you feel about submitting when you are sure you are right?
- Discuss what it means for a leader to let someone else lead?

Everything...
Ephesians 5:24

"*We all learn submission because we all have 'bosses',
whether we're presidents of companies or not. The easiest
place to learn it is in family.* —*Richard Foster*

Principle 23

Submission in crisis ought to be
determined long before the crisis
arrives.

'Everything' is an incredibly big
concept. Let that soak in for a
moment. Pretty overwhelming,
isn't it? You cannot get anymore
comprehensive than 'everything'.
Unfortunately, most couples fail
to recognize the teaching is based on pragmatism, rather than a statement
about equality. Hence, it's crucial to remember the concept of equality
within the Trinity and the consequent need for functional decision-
making. That is, when three equals are present, as in the Trinity, how do
they go about avoiding a debate at every turn (and forget the idea they
always think alike; simply not the case). The answer, of course, resides in
a pragmatic approach by which equal beings determine who will guide
and when. Thus, we have stumbled onto a bit of wisdom every couple
should embrace: *Decide Who Is Going To Drive And When, Long Before It's
Time To Drive.* And wise couples seem to have an innate or intuitive sense
of who should drive and when.

Don often suggests to couples choosing to engage him for their premarital counseling of the utter importance of deciding who will be the
final decision-maker, when hours of prayer and dialogue come up empty,
a divided camp, in the seemingly endless scenarios they will face: money,
housing, child discipline, job location, and on it goes. But regardless of how
well couples prepare, sooner of later, they stumble upon the proverbial,

'worth fighting over' issue, an issue both of you deem so important you are willing to fight, sadly, at all costs. Unless, of course, you have a plan. So comes Paul's divine wisdom.

Still, it's critical to understand the pragmatic nature of Paul's suggestion, rather than attributing his comments to an understanding of one gender better qualified to lead than the other. To the contrary, gender specific guidelines for any area of day-to-day living are typically counterproductive and unhelpful. The uniqueness of each individual determines who is better qualified to lead in any particular set of circumstances. No such thing as men are always better in these circumstances and women in those (really, no such thing!). Every relationship is unique, as are the two people making up the relationship. So do the wise thing and determine who will drive according the skill set needed, long before a certain set of conditions actually appear. In our family, I handle the money, Don handles maintenance, I decorate, etc. Keep in mind, we often discuss the particulars in any given scenario and typically come to consensus, but, sooner or later, a decision has to be made, and when we disagree, the predetermined leader makes the final call. On those rare occasions when we can't talk our way through it, and rare is the case, the predetermined decision maker takes the lead.

Nonetheless, at some point, an unexpected and '*worth fighting for*' issue arrives, and when a predetermined leader for the moment has not been decided, chaos soon climbs in the window. It is in those moments that God provides an alternative approach when consensus simply cannot be found. We often call this principle the 'Divine Coin Toss'. Long ago, God, educated by the wisdom of living in radical equality within the Trinity, recognized there would be moments when two equals genuinely disagree over critical matters (Jesus, in the garden, begging the Father to do this another way); hence, the need for a predetermined system providing a 'how-to' in moments of authentic disagreements regarding critical decisions in life. I'm sure there were multiple options God considered regarding decision-making. Take turns, flip a coin every time, hire a mediator, ask a counselor, etc. But, in the end, God simply declared married couples ought to follow the model of the Trinity, a predetermined decision maker who would bare the responsibility of enduring the consequences of the decisions made; much like an army general who sends troops into battle knowing some will die. Thus, God flipped the proverbial coin (or whatever model God elected) and determined a leader for the most intense moments of disagreement. Fortunately, or unfortunately, depending on your point of view, the coin landed on the female as the partner who would submit to the leadership of her husband. And as you would expect, submission in moments of authentic disagreement is an incredibly difficult role, especially when you are absolutely sure your husband is making the wrong decision! Hence, Paul reminds his readers that this advanced stage of discipleship can only be accomplished by those who are infilled and empowered by the presence of the Holy Spirit.

Ultimately, most wives hit that moment of uncertainty, a decision you deem so critical that surrender and submission seem foolish and unwise. In those moments, you will be tempted to rethink God's challenge in 'everything'. Like Jesus in the Garden, you will agonize as you surrender to the leadership of your spouse, just as Jesus agonized in surrendering to the will of the Father. You may even appear to sweat 'drops of blood' as the agony of self-surrender intensifies.

Don and I have rarely tread on such sacred ground; instead, we have managed to find consensus and uneasy agreement over the course of our almost four decades of marriage. But there have been those rare moments when I surrendered, utterly dependent on God and the unseen wisdom of my husband. Let me confess, I have been unexpectedly and truly amazed at the peace I found when surrendering to his decision, even when still convinced he was wrong. Still, here we are, proclaiming the power of submission, the radical submission of the Trinity, equals still walking together even in the midst of moments of radical disagreements. 'Everything' is an incredibly big concept, even within the Trinity...

Time for coffee and conversation...

- What areas have you decided each one of you should lead in?
- Have there been times in your life when you surrendered knowing you were right?

Action Point...

- Discuss why it is important to know who will lead in what areas.
- Discuss how you intend to lead in times of disagreement.

Husbands love your wives...
Ephesians 5:25

"The gospel alone liberates you to live a life of scandalous generosity, unrestrained sacrifice, uncommon valor, and unbounded courage. — *Tullian Tchividjian*

Principle 24

Love always sacrifices for the sake of the object of love: your spouse. But only after hearing the intent of God.

The challenge to 'love' is the most difficult of all human endeavors, the antithesis of self-interest, the surrendering of all self-preservation, the supreme act of imitation in the trek after Jesus. Scholars have long noted the interesting omission of 'love' in regards to the role of the wife in relationship to her husband in the book of Ephesians; instead, it's replaced with the equally challenging call to 'submit' (respect) rather than 'love'. Of course, submission in many ways is the embodiment of 'love', the challenge to surrender independence, autonomy, self-protection, and self-enhancement for the sake of another. But the challenge to 'love' as Jesus loved takes the concept of submission to extremes, exemplified and modeled in the radical equality of the Trinity, a willingness to follow instructions, to 'die on a cross' for the sake of profoundly broken others. This is the foundation of the challenge to love as Jesus loved.

As difficult as the call to 'submit' is, ladened with a willingness to surrender to the will of another, it pales in comparison to the profound challenge to 'love' as Jesus loved; especially when left with the responsibility to listen carefully for the specifics of what such 'love' will entail toward others. Such is the dilemma for every husband as he embraces the call to love as "...Christ loved the Church and gave Himself up for her." He must first accept the challenge to listen carefully for the will of God regarding the specifics of how to love as Jesus loved. Hearing the particulars of love is a critical first step toward loving as He loved, led by the instruction of God the Father. Hence, no husband loving as Jesus loved would call his wife to any act of submission unless he could confidently suggest, "I think I have heard from God the direction our lives should take." Without an assurance God is leading 'this way,' the best a husband can offer his bride in times of radical disagreement is a heartfelt, "I think we should do this..." And it goes without saying, there is a profound difference in offering your bride, "I sense God leading us in this direction..." and "This is the best I can come up with..." Jesus rested in the assurance He was certain of the direction God was providing. Unfortunately, husbands rarely have that same rock solid certainty, especially when his bride radically disagrees. Hence, it's easy to understand why so many men are hesitant to step up and lead. Hearing from God is a critical first step for any husband calling his wife into a state of submission, a willingness to trust. But if you can't offer her "I'm confident God is leading this way", perhaps you can offer her, "I've prayed and consulted with the Serving King, and this is the direction I sense we should move."

Over these many years of counseling couples in trouble, I have discovered anecdotally a common thread: *Wives in radical disagreement with their husbands, in general, resent surrendering to the leadership of a man who has not spent significant time in conversation and prayer with the Serving King.* Conversely, wives who trust their husband's intimacy with the Serving King find surrendering to his leadership much easier when those moments of radical disagreement arise. In fact, I would suggest, confidence in your husband's communion with God is a key toward enabling brides to surrender to the leadership of a husband. This is simply an essential piece for every husband to comprehend and implement.

Notice the challenge to cleanse her by "...the washing of water with the Word" (more on this in the next section). The term 'Word' suggests an understanding of God's will, God's instruction, God's ways of 'being and doing' as you move forward. God's Word, God's ways of 'being and doing' in the midst of radical disagreement, is the soothing ointment to the soul of a woman who surrenders her autonomy to the leadership of her husband. Therefore, the challenge for every husband is to make sure he is in intimate communion with God, discerning the will of God in the midst of radical disagreement.

Notice, as well, the call of God toward 'self-sacrifice' for the sake of your bride, and eventually your children. The mandate from God is to make sure your bride is surrendering to the sacrificial love of a man who 'gives himself up for her', mimicking the Serving King, surrendering self-protection and enhancement for the sake of his bride. Thus, husbands will soon discover the 'Word' offered by God typically calls for decision-making which always places the health and wholeness of his bride and family ahead of himself. Concern for self always finishes a distant second in the heart of a man communing with the Serving King.

As a husband and follower of the Serving King, I am quick to confess I had the purpose of marriage upside down when I walked down that aisle. I thought Laura was radically committed to making my life better. Little did I know she was thinking the exact same thing about me. We both soon discovered neither would find what we were hoping for. Instead, we were a couple of kids on a path to self-fulfillment, counting on our spouse to make it happen. It didn't. But under the tutorage of a seasoned warrior trekking after the Serving King, I began to understand my role as husband, companion, and leader when necessary. The challenge to 'love' your bride as Christ loved the Church is immense and, more times than not, overwhelming. It, too, requires the infilling and empowering of the Holy Spirit to suppress the ever-present 'self-preservation' mode operational in all human beings. And just as she was called to 'submit' to the immensity of 'everything', so husbands are called to the relentless task of 'gave himself up for her' in each and every moment. Husbands, create an environment of self-sacrifice enabling surrender in the moments of radical disagreement...

Time for coffee and conversation...

- Why does God call men to love as Jesus loved?
- How much easier is it to surrender to a man in intimate relationship with God?

Action Point...

- Discuss the difference between the call to respect and love.
- Tell your spouse why you think they have an intimate relationship with God.

That He might sanctify her, having cleansed her by the
washing of water with the word...
Ephesians 5:26

" *Words are singularly the most powerful force available
to humanity. We can choose to use this force constructively
with words of encouragement, or destructively using words
of despair. Words have energy and power with the ability to
help, to heal, to hinder, to hurt, to harm, to humiliate and
to humble.* —*Yehuda Berg*

Principle 25

Healing is the 'prime directive' for
every marriage.

Early in marriage comes the awareness of 'brokenness', the unwanted caboose of every relationship. You simply cannot avoid exposure to the 'shadow' dimensions your spouse has worked so desperately to conceal. It is the inevitable moment in authentic self-disclosure, or simply the unavoidable 'slip-up' no person can avoid when journeying across a lifetime of togetherness. Sooner or later, you will see the 'shadow', and with that recognition comes the critical moment of every marriage: Now what? Where do we go from here?

Thus, the historical warning in traditional marriage vows, "...for better or worse, for richer, for poorer, in sickness and health, to love and to cherish, until death us do part." It is the reminder of what is to come as you journey together across the messiness of life. And yes, it is the messiness of life which tears downs the walls hiding the 'authentic you'. But, more importantly, the vow reminds us that no 'shadow', regardless of the ugliness of the wound, provides an excuse to abandon the lifelong journey. Instead, recognition of the 'shadow', the brokenness, is nothing more than a point of understanding, an awareness of the job at hand, the challenge to every marriage relationship: *Transformation And Healing*.

Thus, brokenness is never the last word in a thriving marriage relationship; rather, it is a beginning point for transformation, an opportunity to engage in the healing process God intends for every marriage. Once the 'shadow' has been recognized, the challenge to bring about healing begins. But every man and woman seriously engaged in interacting with 'Word' should be warned that the recognition of your spouse's shadow rarely precedes the recognition of your own shadow. Self-awareness is the critical first step in the healing process.

Over the last three decades, I have seldom encountered husbands or wives who comprehend the scope of the cleansing and healing power of God's Word, nor their responsibility to 'know' the Word prior to any effort to fulfill the challenge to be a powerful healing agent for their spouse. Nonetheless, every spouse needs to recognize the dual cleansing occurring in every marriage relationship through encounters with the teaching of God's Word. As you might expect, 'shadow' healing begins in the heart and mind of every spouse long before engaging in the effort to bring transformation and healing to another.

No person can possibly encounter the Word of God in an ongoing, authentic manner without being impacted and transformed by the power of the Word in their own life. Nonetheless, it is the husband who is challenged to mimic Jesus in 'knowing' and 'living' the Word of God in a day-to-day manner, thereby bringing about healing and transformation in his own life and those he touches. The encounter with 'Word' in the life of any person brings about dramatic self-awareness of personal 'shadows' long before recognizing the 'shadow' in a spouse. Thus, no man (person) can unleash the transforming and healing power of God's Word in another without first being touched and transformed by the encounter. Such is the difficult challenge for every husband and wife: *know the Word of God and its transformative power in your own life before moving toward your spouse.*

The challenge to 'sanctify her' (restore to wholeness) is comprehensive, enabling a final presentation "...without spot or wrinkle or any such thing" (more on this in the next section). What is critical to grasp in the healing process is the means by which healing can occur, "...*washing of water with the Word.*" Healing is the by-product of immersion into the wisdom of God's Word. Thus, every husband is challenged to become so familiar with God's Word that it becomes a 'water' by which cleansing occurs both for himself and his bride. Unfortunately, healing too often never occurs as husbands, unfamiliar with the intimacies of Word, are woefully unprepared to deal with the 'shadow' as it appears in their own life and the life of their wife. Thus, the prime directive of marriage, transformation and healing, never occurs; instead, the 'shadow', corrosive when left untreated, whittles away at life's most important relationship, ultimately killing it.

Imagine the willingness of a wounded spouse in following your lead, as she sees the incredible power of God at work in your life bringing about transformation and healing regarding the 'shadow' residing in you. Conversely, when she is in doubt about your encounter with the 'Word', your relationship with the Serving King, your bride, more often than not, will resist your efforts to bring healing to the 'shadows' lurking in the crevices of her life.

Husbands, resist the temptation to abdicate your role as 'knower of Word'. The task is critical for every marriage relationship. 'Word' is the cleansing power toward every 'shadow' lurking in the 'being and doing' of all people, the water by which we are cleansed, healed, and transformed. Left unexposed, 'shadows' slowly nibble away at the extremity of every marriage relationship, relentlessly moving toward the heart, a corrosive agent bent on destruction. Only 'Word' has the power to render every 'shadow' powerless. Husbands, embrace the challenge, "...washing of the water of the Word." Unleash its transforming power...

Time for coffee and conversation...

- Why is it so important to know the Word?
- Do you think bride and groom are equally responsible to know the Word?

Action Point...

- Describe what God has been showing you about yourself as you encounter Word.
- Discuss how each of you might bring about healing and wholeness in your spouse.

He might present the church to Himself
without spot or wrinkle...
Ephesians 5:1

" *The proof of the pudding is in the eating... —Anonymous*

Principle 26

Marriage is the greatest spot
remover to the human condition.

I am always intrigued by the modern reaction when hearing, "We have been married 38 years." Almost without fail, people respond the same way, "Wow!" reflecting the modern ineptitude in marriage. Most folks just can't seem to imagine a couple staying together for almost four decades. Thus, in some sense, moderns equate success in marriage with longevity, and sadly so. Marriage was never intended to be simply a marathon, a never-ending race, a 'come hell or high water affair'; instead, marriage initiates a healing and redemptive process in which human beings evolve into the wholesome people God intended, "... without spot or wrinkle." But, make no mistake, the process can be unpleasant at times, taking longer than most of us expect. Let's face it, we all have lots of spots and wrinkles needing the healing touch of God.

Thus, the ultimate goal for every marriage relationship is not longevity; rather, it is the evolution of each partner into the fullest expression of Godliness: *Sanctification.* Hence, the challenge is to remove every 'spot and wrinkle', precisely because they are there, blemishes hindering the evolution into the image of His Son. And yes, every person has 'spots and wrinkles', regardless of how well they were hidden during the dating process. And the much-needed 'spot remover' can only be found in the intimacy of an authentic, long-term relationship like marriage. Marriage, with its intimate insight, provides the optimum opportunity for 'spot and wrinkle' removal.

Sanctification, 'being', and consequent 'doing' as does the Serving King, liberation from life's 'spots and wrinkles', seems relatively easy in the solitude of the 'single life', a life in which most of the personal 'spots and wrinkles' remain in the proverbial 'blind spot' (chances are you took care of the ones you could see long ago). Marriage provides the much-needed extra set of eyes capable of seeing deep into the 'blind spots' of a spouse's life. Unfortunately, it is the 'spots and wrinkles' rising to the surface within a long-term relationship which easily irritate, creating friction in almost every marriage relationship. Moderns, bewitched by the foolishness of media, interpret 'friction' as the death knoll of a doomed relationship.

Friction can be a healthy aspect of every relationship, providing the opportunity for the imperfections in 'being and doing' to be erased as defective spouses grind away at each other, much like rocks in a tumbler, battering each imperfect partner into the image of the Son, sanctification brought to fruition. It is the friction of authentic relationship that removes the 'spots and wrinkles' for those tenacious enough to withstand the heat!

Nonetheless, terrified by unexpected friction, you will be tempted to run from the inevitable battering within even the richest of marriage relationships. Not understanding the gift of insight provided by your spouse, tired of being battered and ground by the one person in the world you can never fool, the one who knows you intimately, even in the tiniest details, the one who radically loves you like no other, you will interpret their insights as attacks rather than opportunities for growth. And you, equally aware of your spouse's imperfections, will sense the urge to resist the insights of the one God has placed into the most intimate dimensions of your life. Thinking your only option is to fight or flight, you will be tempted to flee, and flee quickly, but there are much better options available.

Sainthood, the final stages of personal development, can never be sustained away from being 'saints together', battered into His image by the imperfections of the one God has equipped for the task at hand, your spouse. It is your spouse who brings about the development of the final stages of 'being and doing' in the ways of the Serving King. Resist the temptation to run when the removal of every 'spot and wrinkle' enters the final stages of personal development.

Here lies the mystery of the process of 'spot and wrinkle' removal within the intimacy of marriage. Those who find sanctification, no 'spots or wrinkles', are those who resist the temptation to run from the realities of an imperfect relationship, the inevitable destination of any relationship with another human being. Instead, choosing to remain in the midst of imperfection, those who journey together are battered into sanctification, 'spot and wrinkle' free, only as they sustain the courage to journey on, fearlessly grinding away.

When Don and I first began our journey together, the 'spots and wrinkles' were glaringly ugly and profound. Sometimes I wonder how we survived those early years as the 'spots and wrinkles' ground against one another. The 'grinding' in those early years was exhausting. By way of confession, let me suggest there were days when both of us wondered, "Is this really what God has in mind? Or did we just choose poorly and need to cut our losses before this gets really ugly?" Fortunately, God provided mentors for both of us in those early days, people who helped us understand the process of living intimately with another flawed human being. Thankfully, we stayed the course and resisted the urge to flee into the night. Soon, we began to reap the harvest of journeying with someone who saw our darkest shadows, our worst 'spots and wrinkles', and stayed. Perfection has not yet arrived for either of us, but we see its shadow breaking just over the horizon...

Time for coffee and conversation...

- Why is sanctification a critical part of our journey into the depth of marriage?
- How does our understanding of each other enable sanctification?
- Why is it so important to understand your spouse is a work in progress?

Action Point...

- Describe a safe way to discuss those spots and wrinkles.
- Discuss how you might assist each other in moving toward sanctification.

In the same way...
Ephesians 5:28

"*I am a member of a team, and I rely on the team, I defer to it and sacrifice for it, because the team, not the individual, is the ultimate champion.*** ***—Mia Hamm***

Principle 27

Radical self-sacrifice is the essential foundation of every transformational relationship.

Marriage begins and ends with sacrifice, the means by which authentic healing and wholeness can be found. Unfortunately, few are willing to sustain the price of 'sacrifice', fatiguing of the cost, soon cozying up to slothfulness, initiating the decaying process, robbing too many marriages of the vitality God intended. Tragically, the many, while aware of the stench of decay, are content to whittle the years away, until the stench of decay is no longer offensive. So comes the quiet, slow death of far too many marriage relationships joining the ranks of the 'walking dead', lifeless marriages held together by threads strained to the limits. But there is a better way, another way, the way of the Serving King... Self-sacrifice is not nearly so rare as the many would have you to believe. To the contrary, it happens on a daily basis across a broad spectrum of relationships and activities, from sports to marriage, and everything in between. Thus, it may be important to ask the question, "What drives people to radical self-sacrifice in the ordinary relationships of day-to-day living?" For Mia Hamm and the United States Women's Soccer Team, it was the dream of a World Championship, better yet, an Olympic Gold Medal. With the goal in mind, they made incredible sacrifices for one another, all in a gargantuan effort to secure the prize. The prize, kept in view, motivates us beyond the momentary pain of sacrifice.

Most couples entering into marriage do so because they believe in the prize, the joy of a relationship providing some of life's most cherished prizes: *Relational And Physical Intimacy.* Unfortunately, once the prize is tarnished, perhaps even lost in the immediate moment and condition, the desire to stay engaged quickly disappears, simply because too many folks think the 'tarnished prize' can never be restored to its original condition. To the contrary, like a bone that has mended from a break, making it stronger than prior to the break, tarnished marriages often gain a luster brighter than ever before. The key is to remain engaged as God heals and restores even the most damaged relationships. Restored luster is a first fruit of God's presence. Restoration is what God does best.

Sacrifice for another, the ultimate gift of love, rarely thrives for long periods of time unrewarded. And relational rewards are often slow in developing within a marriage. Thus, in order for ongoing sacrifice to occur, another stimuli is needed. Jesus relied on His relationship with God, His love for the Father, to empower His relentless commitment to enhance the lives of those He loved. Ultimately, it was His love for the Father, and a consequent love of who and what the Father loved, that sustained Jesus across His sacrificial lifetime and ministry; thus comes Paul's challenge to "...in the same way." Only your sustained love relationship with God will empower you to love your spouse "...in the same way" sacrificially.

On more than one occasion across the years, I have arrived at that disparaging moment of disengagement, a lack of desire to continue, the well of self-sacrifice virtually dried up. In those moments, it has been the quiet voice of the ever-present 'Coach' who has sustained me and provided the impetus to carry on for one more day, one more moment, one more act of engagement, even when the well was dry. I continue, even to this day, to hear His quiet voice suggesting, "We can do this! Trust me, a championship is just around the corner." And indeed it was.

At some point along the way of self-sacrifice, you will begin to ask questions regarding the ultimate goal of every marriage relationship, "What does a championship look like? How do I know we are winning? What am I sacrificing for?" And no, longevity is never the ultimate goal. Winning is never about simply not divorcing. God has something much more significant in mind. God envisions a relationship in which a family unit thrives and prospers both as a 'team' and as individuals.

A championship in a marriage relationship reflects an environment in which each individual thrives and prospers across a broad spectrum of concerns: intimacy, depth of relationship, physical health, children, personal accomplishments, etc. And success in each of those areas will require personal sacrifice over and over again. Sacrificing for each other's success becomes the foundation upon which every marriage relationship moves toward a championship.

I sometimes imagine those final moments for Jesus as He hung upon that cross, asking the question I often ask in the throes of self-sacrifice, "Father, is this really going to make a difference in the long run? Are Our children really going to respond to My offering, My self-sacrifice?" I suspect His Father responded, "Stick with it, Son, the championship is just around the corner."

I have been blessed across the decades to join in the raucous celebration of multiple championships, teammates shouting and celebrating, slapping each other on the back, high fives, tears of joy, as the 'team', each individual, basked in the moment of success. Not a single championship arrived without much personal sacrifice from each player. It simply is the way of a championship effort. Likewise, great marriage championships are the culmination of two individuals engaging "...in the same way" sacrificially, for the sake of the team. Rest assured, there will be days, especially on the backside of loss, when you will wonder, "Is this really going to make a difference?" Listen carefully, as the Father utters once again, "Stick with it, the championship is just around the corner."

Time for coffee and conversation...

- Why is sacrifice a critical piece of every marriage?
- What does a championship marriage look like in your mind?
- Can you identify any couples you think have won a championship?

Action Point...

- Describe what a championship looks like to your spouse?
- Do the two of you have the same championship image in mind?

Love their wives as their own bodies...
Ephesians 5:31

" *Take care of your body. It's the only place you have to live.* —*Jim Rohn*

Principle 28

Take care of yourself before attempting to care for others.

Paul's words strike us as oddly out of place. Nonetheless, you have probably been on the airplane as the steward instructs you on how to survive an emergency, "Please place the oxygen mask on your own face before attempting to assist your child." It serves as a reminder to us that no one can provide sustained care and attention in a relational war zone, if they are in a weakened condition themselves, especially in a long-term relationship like marriage. Conversely, those who first provide for their own physical and emotional health are much better prepared for assisting others over the long haul. And marriage, more than any other relationship we experience, is a long-term give and take. And as you might expect, the give and take is rarely equal over the short-term.

Like many couples, Don and I really struggled with this principle early in our relationship. Neither of us was particularly good at releasing the other to pursue interests enjoyable and rewarding for the other. Don still loved to play basketball with the guys, and I enjoyed shopping and hanging out with the girls. But, for some reason, perhaps our own insecurities or selfishness, neither of us genuinely released the other to go and enjoy their particular interests. The result was not pretty and did much to damage our relationship in those early days. Only later did we both begin to understand how important it was to allow each other to continue experiencing activities and interests the other may not enjoy. To this day, Don still loathes shopping, even for himself, and early on I banned him from sharing that delightful experience with me. We have been happier ever since.

Thus, two dimensions are critically important for this aspect of married life to flourish. First, recognize your partner is who they are because of the way they lived prior to marrying you. Hence, for them to continue being the person you love, the person you wanted to marry, you will need to recognize the value of the activities making your partner who they are. Demand they abandon activities making them who they are, and you run the risk of robbing your partner of vitality and enthusiasm needed for life and marriage. Thus, each of you will need to recognize the value of releasing your partner to enjoy those activities helping to shape and form your spouse into the person you love. It is those activities and interests that provide the vitality and life flowing out of your partner toward you. It truly is a win/win for you both.

But there is a second principle you will have to equally embrace. Once you have been released to 'care for your own body' and soul, do just that, actually 'care for your own body.' And sustaining your body, and emotional health, rarely gets easier as the years roll by. In fact, with each passing year, body and emotional health become more and more difficult to create and sustain. Like most things in life, you will have to be very intentional about nurturing your body and soul.

Because Don and I have so few activities and interests we both genuinely enjoy (movies, beach vacations and travel!), this practice has been critical for us to enact. Don still enjoys extreme hiking, skiing, and anything involving competition. I, on the other hand, still enjoy shopping, coffee with friends, and my favorite, hanging with my singing group. Thus, we really have needed to turn each other loose to enjoy those dimensions of life that feed each other's soul and body.

But there is a critical aspect to turning your partner loose to enjoy life: *A Payoff For Your Partner.* I have discovered over the years, Don rarely vetoes any activity I want to engage in, including being away from home while hanging out with my girlfriends. Truth be told, he digs the alone time, really enjoys having time to himself. But it is more than that. I work very hard to make sure he is the focus of my attention when I return home. He reaps the benefits of my time away, always receiving a payoff for allowing me to engage in activities he prefers to avoid. The payoff is essential to encouraging independence, personal care and development. Again, the proverbial win/win for both of us.

As Jim Rohn suggested, body health is essential; it really is the only place you have to live, to experience life, to engage with vigor and gusto. Unfortunately, life has a way of whittling away our enthusiasm for soul and body care. And as we drift farther and farther away from healthy bodies and souls, so does our ability to facilitate care for those we love most in life. Hence, Paul's call to 'care for our bodies' is a reminder to stay in the game, committed to a healthy lifestyle, able to care for those we love. An unhealthy body and soul radically reduces your ability to provide for those you love most.

As the years go on, resist the temptation to become satisfied with a lifestyle that wars against a healthy body and soul; especially, when both of you are tempted to slip into a pattern requiring very little from either of you. In a very short time, life will become a drudgery at worst, and a bore at its very best. Turn the TV off, put down your electronic distraction, and join your spouse in living a healthy, sustainable lifestyle. You will discover meeting the needs of your spouse is so much easier when you actually feel good, both physically and deep within your being. As Paul suggested, put the same energy into caring for your spouse as you have infused into your own physical and emotional well being. Truth be told, that is going to happen no matter what. Your partner can never receive anymore than your physical and emotional being will allow. Take seriously the challenge to care for yourself and those you love most...

Time for coffee and conversation...

- Why care for yourself first?
- What do you do to care for your body and soul?
- What does your spouse do to care for their body and soul?

Action Point...

- Describe for your spouse those activities you want to remain a part of your life.
- Describe for your spouse the activities you think they need to keep a part of life.

∽

CHAPTER 5

Love For A Lifetime

Sustain the Primacy Of The Marriage

Y OU WOULD THINK the primacy of marriage goes without saying, common sense if you will, but let us assure you, it is not. The distractions of life will soon crowd out the primacy of the marriage relationship, unless each spouse is radically committed to sustaining it as a top priority, especially after the children arrive and careers have kicked into gear. Moderns, thinking their delay in marriage until school and careers are completed and well established, will believe they have discovered the key (delayed marriage) to sustaining the primacy of the marriage relationship. But they have not. Life simply has a way of throwing distractions of every kind your way, even without kids or careers, across the many decades of married life. The only thing that changes is the nature of the distraction. Life just finds a way to distract at any age. Making your relationship with your spouse the primary focus of your life will challenge you to the limits.

But the dating portion of every relationship models for each couple a foundational principle providing direction for every phase of married life: *The Primacy Of Relationship With Your Significant Other* (now that you are married, your spouse). Typically, couples are relentless in making sure the dating relationship is the primary focus of life (perhaps, thinking it will be only necessary while trying to secure the invitation to marriage, a tragic mistake with dire consequences down the road).

Inevitably, in a high percentage of the couples I work with, someone will suggest, "Don, that just isn't realistic, sometimes other priorities take precedent." Well, of course, they do; hence, what we are talking about is as simple as making sure the cycles of life always leave room for couple time, couple interests, and couple development.

My mother and father well understood the critical role the primacy of the marriage relationship played in a long-lasting marriage. More importantly, perhaps, they set practical guidelines for just how long any marriage relationship ought to take second seat to the other pressing needs in life: never more than one year. It was a principle they never spoke of to me directly, never wrote about in a letter, never identified as a principle for every married couple; instead, they simply made sure Laura and I never went more than 52 weeks without getting a break from life and childcare. Each and every year, they would find a way to relieve us of childcare duties and life in general, even providing funding if we needed it to get away. Neither of us had a clue what these two seasoned vets were up to, not until years later when it finally dawned on us what the wise sages were passing on to their now grown children: *Make sure you focus on your marriage in a significant manner each and every year.* We still, even as I'm typing these words while hiding in Mexico, find a week or two every year just to focus on each other.

It was in the early days of our learning to 'vacation' as a couple that we discovered just how easy it was to disengage, unintentionally, as a couple. Our first 24 hours of every getaway were often traumatic as we tried to figure out, "Now what? What should we do with all this alone time?"

One of our favorite "Everybody Loves Raymond" episodes (yep, an oldie most of you have never seen) demonstrates the principle well. Ray and Debra finally get a night out without the children, a night to share a romantic dinner together. It doesn't take very long for them to discover they have virtually nothing to talk about other than: the bread is really good, the butter is just the right room temperature, endless kid stories, and old life stories they have both heard a hundred times. The evening is a total bust as the two of them panic over how little they have to talk about anymore. Gone are conversations about future dreams and desires, intimate whisperings, and where life is leading. It is a pretty dismal state of affairs for them both. Sadly, the sitcom is so hilariously funny, because many of us, perhaps most of us, fall into that same damaging pattern of focusing on everything in life but each other.

But a couple of weeks a year, spread out over 4-6 months, is never enough to genuinely keep your relationship with your spouse up-to-date, vibrant, and stimulating. So comes the challenge to figure out how you will go about making each other an ongoing day-to-day, week-to-week, priority in your life. Laura and I have found a few little tricks that seem to work for us. These are not prescriptive, rather just descriptive, of what works for us:

- Intimacy: Physical and emotional intimacy are a crucial piece of significant relationships. We are very careful not to allow too much time to pass (you will have to figure out how much time that is) before we are together both physically and emotionally. It can become mechanical at times, but intimacy is an essential component in remaining close.
- Coffee: Whether at home or at a local coffee shop, Laura and I try to grab a cup of coffee together at least every couple days. It provides us with a much-needed debriefing time as we catch up on each other's life.
- Walks together: Early on, we discovered we talk best when on the move. Thus, long walks together are a part of our regime. Hence, our love for the beach and its endless miles just right for walking and talking.
- The same bed time: At some point, we realized how important it was to head for the bedroom at the same time. Rarely do we

actually fall asleep at the same time, but we are in bed together at the same time every evening. This nightly cuddle time provides a much-needed get reacquainted time every evening.

- <u>Laughter before sleep</u>: I'm not sure where or how we discovered this little jewel, but, wow, does it seem to work. Every night, yes, every night, we cuddle in bed together and laugh as we watch our favorite sitcoms over and over again. Laughter provides a powerful bond.

You will have to find strategies for yourself. But, rest assured, without them your relationship will not remain the top priority of your life. In the pages to follow, you will explore the last phase of relationship building: *Becoming and Sustaining Oneness As A Married Couple.*

Leave and Cleave
Ephesians 5:31

"All changes, even the most longed for, have their melancholy; for what we leave behind is a part of ourselves; we must die to one life before we can enter into another!

—Gail Sheehy

Principle 29

Create your own family traditions and rituals.

Perhaps, one of the most challenging dimensions of 'becoming one' is the abandonment of the lifestyle that shaped you. For us that reality appeared without having to think about it. Our first few months unfolded uneventfully as we lived in my parents' basement. Newly married and visitors in my parents' home, we had little opportunity to set up our home. But things would soon change radically. Four months into our marriage, I accepted a call into full-time Christian ministry, dropping out of Drexel University, abandoning my electrical engineering studies, packing up most of our earthly belongings, and driving 2,500 miles across the United States to begin a new career as a student and pastor. Life would never be the same.

Laura and I quickly discovered we came from very different ethnic backgrounds and family traditions. Laura is 100% Italian (yep, the DNA test just confirmed it), right down to talking with her hands at all times. I was a southern mongrel, transplanted to New Jersey as a teenager, unaware of what lay ahead as my bride and I began the quest into marriage. Our move to Idaho would soon release the tension of attempting to merge two very different ways of family life into our way of being and doing as newly-minted Minters.

Trouble arose as soon as the unpacking began. I love balance and symmetry, to a fault. Worse yet, I love functionality, design that enhances function. Laura, on the other hand, has little concern for function or symmetry. She lives by one guiding principle, "Is is pretty and does it make me feel good when I walk in the room?" The battleground would soon be apparent as we attempted to set up shop in the kitchen. Mr. Functionality and Mrs. Does It Look Pretty would soon be at war, and no family referee within 2,000 miles; a real blessing, though neither of us knew it at the time. The problem, of course, was that we brought our prior family lifestyles and values into the marriage, each expecting the other to surrender quickly once acquainted with a better way of doing things. Unfortunately, neither saw the wisdom of an alternative approach, nor surrendered. Mr. Functionality and Mrs. Does It Look Pretty soon battled into the night over beautiful counters that made the creation of a peanut butter and jelly sandwich almost impossible. Some 40 years later, we will still squabble from time to time as functionality and aesthetics come to blows. Amazing how little things change in the midst of all the change.

But the real battle lay looming in the distance, the drama of Christmas, the decision on how to unwrap presents once our children had arrived. Laura's family celebrated Christmas as an ode to 'Santa', every unwrapped present appearing around the Christmas tree from good old St. Nick. My family gave Santa a nod, one unwrapped and assembled gift from the bearded one, while the rest were given from somebody to somebody. Once again, battle lines were drawn as family traditions from a prior life clashed as our new family members arrived.

Without much fanfare, Laura and I soon recognized a new way of being and doing needed to rise up from our rich family experiences. And, indeed, they did, though not without unanticipated drama. The kitchen soon became a beautifully functional one. Pretty pots and pans that were highly functional as well. Even the can opener was stylish and cute. As for Christmas, a merger of our family traditions soon appeared. Santa delivered one unwrapped and assembled gift on Christmas morning. Name tags on all the remaining wrapped gifts. And the highlight of our family gathering was the privilege of opening one gift, chosen by each member of the family on Christmas Eve. A new tradition with which neither of us had any prior experience. A new 'Minter' way of doing Christmas.

But the Scriptural admonition has a much greater significance than simply providing the impetus for creating new family traditions. More important is the warning to avoid creating ongoing alliances with people who will typically, ok, maybe always, line up with you in times of crisis. In a healthy family unit, mom and dad have always been your biggest allies, and maybe even to an extreme with the modern era of helicopter parents. Hence, God's warning to 'leave' those alliances as you begin a new journey with your spouse. But it is more than just leaving, it is the matter of 'cleaving' as well. Literally bonding yourself to your spouse in the most intense and intimate manner possible, a cleaving so profound the two shall become one. The evolution of new family liturgies, ways of doing things, can assist the two of you in becoming one.

The formation of your own family lifestyle is a critical part of the cleaving process. It creates the liturgies of family life identifying you as a couple, and later as a family. These liturgies are an essential part of what it will mean to be a part of your clan. As you begin your journey together, explore creative ways to symbolize your uniqueness as a couple, as a family. Don't hesitate to look outside your clan as you consider how to 'be and do' as a family unit. Feel free to consider how other people engage and then adopt those traditions, those ways of being and doing as part of your own tradition. We soon discovered our favorite food on Thanksgiving was not the beloved turkey but Laura's amazing lasagna. Our boys eagerly return home annually to harvest Mom's Thanksgiving Lasagna. And yes, every Christmas Eve, we still pick one special gift to open before the chaos of Christmas morning. It is just the Minter way of doing things...

Time for coffee and conversation...

- Why do unique family traditions matter for each family?
- What family traditions would you like to install from your historical family?
- What family traditions would you like to remove from your historical family?

Action Point...

- Discuss with your spouse traditions you would like to create.
- Discuss with your spouse traditions you would like to import.

The two shall become one flesh.
Ephesians 5:31

"*In love the paradox occurs that two beings become one and yet remain two.***

*—Erich Fromm***

Principle 30

Oneness blossoms as two unique beings embrace guiding values and ways of doing.

Unique to the Christian view of God is its understanding of Trinity: one God, three in person. The doctrine creates the framework for two people becoming 'one' yet functioning at the highest levels as independent entities, equally engaged in similar ways of 'being and doing'.

As a child growing up, I was continually confounded by the unity my mother and father modeled. Countless times I would approach one or the other with a question only to be befuddled by their common reply, "What did your mother say?" or its twin, "What did your father say?" It was the ongoing reality of their commitment to unity, especially when it came to dealing with me and my brother. Their common front was almost impossible to penetrate. Even more amazing was their unanimity when finally forced to answer without being able to consult with the other. Inevitably, their answers were eerily similar, almost as if they had actually chatted, a shocking congruency from these two people who had seemingly pulled it off... become one. My brother and I eventually gave up, knowing these two could not be divided in their fundamental approach to rearing us.

The oneness of the Trinity suggests a way of 'being and doing' so engrained in each person of the Godhead that they function as one entity, even while obviously separated into three beings, engaged fully in three distinct roles: Father, Son and Holy Spirit. Thus, oneness points to more than simply 'one being'; more importantly, oneness suggests a common way of both 'being and doing'. Both factors are critically important in creating oneness mimicking the Trinity.

The New Testament often speaks of the Body of Christ as a single unit, melded together by each person's reception of the Holy Spirit. Much like the Godhead, the indwelling presence of the Holy Spirit provides a unifying reality for the people of God. His unifying presence is intensified in the marriage relationship as each partner experiences the power and presence of the Holy Spirit. The New Testament uses a powerful term to describe our relationship with the Spirit and with our marriage partner: gnosis (knowing). The term is used to describe intimacy between a man and woman (intercourse) as well as the relationship between the Holy Spirit and each individual. Hence, there is a powerful bonding mechanism at work when a man and woman experience intimacy. But for the Christian, there is more at work. The Spirit of the living God is at work uniting a man and woman together via their physical union as the Spirit of God is united by encountering Himself in the 'other'. Like the Trinity itself, the marriage relationship reflects a trinitarian emphasis: Husband, Wife, and the Holy Spirit. He is the Divine Third within the relationship. It is a profound mystery which the Apostle Paul attempted to describe in Ephesians 5:31-32: "Therefore a man shall leave his father and mother and the two shall become one flesh. This is a profound mystery, and I am saying that it refers to the Christ and the Church." Just as the Church functions as a single unit with countless members, so a thriving marriage relationship becomes one as the two are united physically and metaphysically. The Holy Spirit serves as a powerful bonding agent as two individuals are merged into one.

Additionally, the unity of the Trinity is comprehensive, including a 'oneness' of purpose and being, synchronized within the Godhead, enabling each to engage in separate activities all fulfilling the intended common purposes of the Godhead. Likewise, in the marriage relationship: *a man and woman who have been meshed into a single entity soon begin to reflect a common 'being and doing'.* They begin to think and act alike, not in the sense of identical thoughts, rather thinking and acting rising up out of a shared consciousness, a like-mindedness providing purpose and direction for life.

In the latter stages of the development of oneness, an uncanny similarity begins to take shape, almost unconsciously, as husband and wife begin to reflect the 'being and doing' of their partner. They have become one in the midst of their great diversity. Two independent beings who have begun to function as a single unit.

After almost four decades of sharing life together, Laura and I have arrived at that scary point in the richest of marriage relationships, that awkward moment when you can with great certainty finish each other's sentences. Frequently, one of us will share a thought with the other only to hear, "I was just thinking that!"

Now, here is the best part about becoming one: *the process never ends as we are continually evolving into different human beings.* Earlier I suggested, I have been married to at least seven different women, each one of them named Laura Minter. Believe it or not, I'm watching as an eighth version of my wife is taking shape. This version, an incredibly gracious and kind woman, has added a depth of being I am delighted to encounter. She continues to explore dimensions of life I never imagined would catch her interest. She has turned into a bit of a health nut, loves politics and, most shocking of all, even ventured into the "Walking Dead" with her boys at Universal Studios last month! Our youngest son declared, "I can't believe Mom just did that!!!" Frankly, I couldn't believe it either. Who is this woman arriving late in the game of marriage? Later that day, she would be riding roller coasters (a never-gonna-happen event in earlier versions of my bride) and screaming with laughter as we clanked along the rails. And so, becoming one is a never-ending adventure, as God continues to transform you into the person God would have you to be. Hang on tight, the two of you will become more in your oneness than you ever dared to dream or imagine on life's rollercoaster...

Time for coffee and conversation...

- What does it mean to become one?
- How does that oneness continue to evolve?

Action Point...

- Discuss with your spouse the things in life that make you feel closest to them.
- Discuss with your spouse dreams that you've not dared to share thus far.

...let each one of you love his wife
and the wife respect her husband.
Ephesians 5:31

"*Men are born chasers. Women love to be chased. It is the way God created us. Ladies, put on your high heels and let's go! Just remember to let him catch you every now and then...*
—*Laura Minter*

Principle 31

Marriage is a two-sided coin: Love
and Respect / Male and Female.

Much is often made concerning gender roles, both pro and con, and for good reason. As modern culture attempts to banish gender roles as nothing more than 'cultural constructions', randomly created to serve the culture's perceived needs, pushback has begun attempting to emphasize clear distinctions between men and woman arising from more than just cultural desires. Truth be told, there appears to be a few 'hard-wired' dimensions within the male and female DNA codes. And not surprisingly, those dimensions appear over and over again across cultural lines, sometimes even ignoring the whims of the culture. There may indeed be something to the idea of male and female.

Laura constantly reminds me, usually after I have complained a bit about her lack of prowess when it comes to 'chasing me', that women are meant to be pursued, not the other way around. I typically grimace and fuss but to no avail. I have yet to persuade her we ought to swap roles for a trial run. So after whining for a bit, I do indeed lace up my sneakers as her high heels fly down the sidewalk, and the chase begins afresh over and over again.

Interestingly, the Apostle Paul made a clear distinction between how men and woman approach each other at a profoundly basic level. His words are not meant to suggest "Men only love" and "Woman only respect;" rather, these are propensities often appearing in men and women. Specifically, men typically genuinely want to be respected by their brides. Conversely, women really do respond well to a man who will lay down his life for his wife and family. These are powerful tools within the male and female framework.

But Paul's words are not intended to be the 'final words' on husband-wife relationships, instead, reminders to really understand what matters to your spouse. In our case, Laura really does want to know that I am profoundly 'in love' with her and would be willing to sacrifice anything to win her. Conversely, I really do want to know that Laura trusts me when push comes to shove, when difficult decisions have to be made, when life has to be conquered. But it is much more complicated than simple concepts like 'love' and 'respect'.

Early in our marriage, during one of those seasons of difficulty, Laura continually tried to reassure me that things were ok, that she really loved me, really wanted to continue on with me as her husband. As an example of why she loved me so much, she continued to offer, "You are such a great father to our children!" Now, here is the interesting thing, I really didn't care about her thinking I was a great father. I wanted her to want me like she did long before the children ever arrived. I needed her to 'want me', not my functionality as a provider and dad. She was offering me 'respect' as a husband and dad, when what I really wanted was her devotion to me as a virile and attractive male. I quickly discovered, as well, that Laura wanted me to think she was beautiful, really beautiful, a desirable woman, the woman I couldn't live without. Both of us began to understand we had to figure out what 'love' and 'respect' looked like to each other. Love and respect are typically custom-built for the person you are living with.

In the end, what we discovered was the 'hardwiring' was indeed present in each of us. Nonetheless, that 'hardwiring' didn't operate in neat, predictable ways; instead, it manifested itself in very unique ways as the two of us grew up male and female in our historical family environment. Further, as we mingled with the culture at-large, our 'hardwiring' evolved into a way of being that was uniquely us. There were no 'cookie-cutter' techniques for discovering what my 'maleness' or her 'femaleness' really wanted as it pertained to love and respect. Instead, we were forced to discover what love and respect would look like in our unique relationship.

I learned as the years passed by that my loving Laura was radically enhanced by simply telling her how beautiful she was each and every day, multiple times, surrounded by an abundance of the equally important "I love you." Laura has learned my profound need to be desired by her. It is what respect looks like at the most fundamental level in our relationship. We have pieced together the real-life expressions of the two-sided coin of every marriage relationship: love and respect.

I am writing the final words to this book after a long, long, long walk on the beach in Rocky Point, Mexico. After strolling barefoot down three miles of beach, we paused to turn homeward at a man-made jetty. The turnaround spot had collected a large amount of trash including an abandoned plastic bag. Laura had been wanting to pick up trash as we walked along each day. At our feet was a plastic trash bag. She grabbed the bag, quickly filled it with beer cans laying along the beach, and handed it to me to carry back down three miles of beach!

And that about sums it up. Take a bullet for my bride, easy. Carry the stinking bag of beer cans down three miles of beach, ugh! There you have it. Marriage thrives when we determine to carry each other's trash down life's long haul. And just as we crawled back up to our condo, she smiled, thanked me for carrying the bag of trash, and her seashells pulling down the back of my shorts as they bounced around in my pocket. I smiled, grabbed her hand, and off to the pool for a refreshing dip in the water and the rewards yet to come...

Time for coffee and conversation...

- What does 'respect' look like in your relationship?
- What does 'love' look like in your relationship?
- Why do you need both love and respect from your spouse?

Action Point...

- Discuss with your spouse how you might show respect.
- Discuss with your spouse how you might show love.

Don and Laura Minter

Don and Laura have been married for nearly 39 years. Their journey began as high school sweethearts and the love story continues on. Don often suggests, "If we had known marriage was so much fun we wouldn't have waited so long to get married!" Surprising, considering they were married at 19 and 18, respectively. Don attended Drexel University in downtown Philadelphia before transferring to Northwest Nazarene University in Nampa, Idaho, where he earned a BA in Philosophy and Religion, followed by seminary in Kansas City (Master of Divinity) and concluding with a Dr. of Ministry in 2006. He has pastored in a variety of settings from the heart of downtown Phoenix, the back roads of a rural farm community in Missouri, beautiful mountains of Arizona, the coastal beauty of Oregon, and southern hospitality of South Carolina.

Their children, Dustin (36), Derek (32), and the late surprise, Michael Wayne (12), have filled their lives with joy, trauma, and drama (sound like any other parents out there?). They absolutely love to travel, network with people trekking after Jesus, and stay busy whenever possible. Both can be hyperactive, exhausting at times, but fun is always to be found. And both enjoy interacting with the internet and its vast array of communication possibilities.

Laura, an executive assistant, spent much of her career as Vice President Dan Quayle's personal assistant. She continues to work, write, sing, and raise their late surprise Michael. Don loves to write, search for adventure and spend time over coffee with God's people. Both are more passionate about trekking after Jesus than at any point in their lives. Anxious for God's tomorrow in the adventure of life as the journey after Him continues...

As this book winds down, you may be thinking, "What's next? Where do we go from here?" Let us suggest two books for continued reading written by the husband and wife team, John and Stasha Eldridge: Wild At Heart and Captivating. Wild At Heart will introduce females to the wildness of the male spirit, and Captivating will introduce males to the secrets of a woman's heart. Both books will provide you with helpful insights into what may be the 'hardwiring' of your spouse, their God-given generic way of 'being and doing'.

Additional books by Donald Minter

Mornings With Oswald
More Mornings With Oswald
40 Days Deep
Chasing God
More Chasing God

~

If your travels take you to Flagstaff, Arizona,
please stop by FlagNaz
(A Church of the Nazarene) and say hello.

Don and Laura are available to speak at your
next function. You can contact them at:
revminter@me.com